GW00567987

Farewell,
My Lovely

Farewell, My Lovely

A heart-warming collection
of tributes
to dear, departed pets

Compiled by
Susie Cornfield

Illustrations by
Sara Rapoport

Foreword by
HRH The Duchess of Cornwall

GARRET
BOOKS

Farewell, My Lovely

Extended hardback edition published 2009 by Garret Books Ltd

ISBN 978-0-9552279-4-3

First edition published in paperback September 2006 by Garret Books Ltd

reprinted December 2006

Copyright © Susie Cornfield

Illustrations copyright © Sara Rapoport

Garret Books Ltd, Company Registration Number: 5647052

Registered address: Suite 210 Maddison House, 226 High Street, Croydon CR9 1DF, Surrey, UK

www.garretbooks.com

A CIP catalogue record for this book is available from the British Library.

Designed and typeset by Caroline and Roger Hillier, The Old Chapel Graphic Design

www.theoldchapelivinghoe.com

Copy Editor: Ros Lavine

Printed and bound in the UK by CPI Mackays, Chatham ME5 8TD

*In loving memory of
my parents, Roy and Florence Cooper, and Bob,
Dilys Powell and Spike,
Sylvia Myers, the swan of Liverpool,
and Dorene and Andreas Christou, who happily shared
their fruit and veg with any creature that crawled, climbed
or flew into their garden to get it.*

Farewell, My Lovely is a tribute to
Brains the MagnifiCat,
and to the animals who have left
their mark on these pages
and a place in someone's heart.
It's also for your pet,
and for you.

Also by the author

Fiction

Green Fire; a satirical thriller, second in the series, The Chronicles of
Dekaydence (Garret Books, 2009, ISBN 978-0-9552279-3-6).

Black Light; a satirical thriller, first in the series, The Chronicles
of Dekaydence (Garret Books, 2008, ISBN 978-0-9552279-2-9),
published originally as *The Sticky Rock Café*.

Non-fiction

Farewell, my Lovely; a collection of tributes to much-loved departed
pets. Original paperback (Garret Books, 2006,
ISBN 978-0-9552279-1-2).

History

The Queen's Prize; the story of the National Rifle Association of Great
Britain (Pelham Books, 1987, ISBN 0-7207-1751-5).

Contents

Standard UK and US spelling is used, where appropriate.
Any other spelling is down to the author.

☆ 12 ☆

The relationship between ourselves and our fellow creatures is a source of great mystery. Why is it a crawling baby will go after a cat and hug it tight? Why is it a dog will often put up with the indignity of having its tail pulled by a child too young to know better? Why do children and old people derive such comfort and joy from stroking a pet.

Maybe all this is because we feel that these are our companions in this world, that they are sentient creatures, who respond as we do to affection. Somehow we know we share our time on earth with them. They reassure us that we are not alone. They bring us huge joys and we are grateful to them for that.

The tributes in this book are about grieving and loss, but they are much more about gratitude for a moment shared, or a life shared.

Some of our greatest writers, William Shakespeare, DH Lawrence and Ted Hughes amongst them, have captured the nature of this complex coexistence. But even they cannot demystify the nature of this relationship. Look into the eye of a horse or a dog or a goldfish and we know that what is between us is unfathomable. They are our friends through life. That's all we know.

Camilla

Foreword to the first edition

I still remember the last day in the life of Finnegan, the Irish water spaniel and the friend of my childhood. I spent hours crying and tickling his tummy as he sprawled on his back on the sitting-room floor. Later that day he was taken to the vet's for the last time.

Luckily, nobody told me, "He was only a dog." Only a dog . . . only a being, who offered unconditional love, silent listening and complete acceptance. Nobody said that even more hurtful remark – "Get another one." As if dogs were like cars. As if you could just go out and buy a newer model.

As the *Daily Telegraph*'s pet agony aunt I often receive letters from people who are locked into an almost suicidal grief and anger at the loss of an animal friend. It has usually been made worse by somebody telling them they should not be grieving. Occasionally, they have told themselves that their grief is excessive. Yet it must be natural to grieve at the loss of a good friend. Sometimes I think the relationship between a human and an animal is closer than the friendship between human and human. It is a love without words and therefore without lies.

The loss of an animal friend is a real bereavement, whatever unthinking people may say. I send a sympathy card if somebody writes to me about the death of a pet, as a mark of respect for their pain. When we have lost an animal, our grief should be understood and permitted, rather than mocked or discounted.

This book pays tribute to the relationship between animals and their humans. It gives those who read it permission to grieve in their turn. The stories are a memorial to the happiness that we have enjoyed with our animals.

Celia Haddon, May 2006

Celia Haddon is currently studying for a degree in animal behaviour.

Introduction

When my feline companion of some 16 years died, I was devastated. But it was only when people began sharing with me their tales of love and loss of an animal that it struck me that a collection of these stories might help people through their grief. I also realised it'd be a fitting tribute to my little cat, Brains, who'd brought me so much fun, friendship and love, and had claimed permanent residence in my heart.

The first edition of *Farewell, my Lovely* was published in paperback in 2006. It might've stopped there but its modest success led to us being advised that rather than a reprint we create a more enduring hardback edition. A daring and unusual move! It made me think it'd be rather nice to extend the book with stories from around the world. And here it is: the original, with many more tales – and poems and prose – from loving pet owners. And even more delightful drawings from my dear friend, the artist Sara Rapoport.

True, these are stories of loss but equally, as with the first edition, they are stories of the joy, fun and love that an animal can bring into our lives. I'd hoped to do more stories – from more countries, about different animals – but time, and tears, intervened. Perhaps variety doesn't matter. Because, as we all know, the experience of loving and losing an animal is not bounded by age, gender or race or fur, fin or feather.

I hope you enjoy the tales, old and new, included in this extended hardback edition of *Farewell, My Lovely* and that if you are suffering an animal bereavement this book helps you sail more comfortably through the rough waters of your loss, enabling you to recognise that however much your pet gave you, you gave your pet much in return. A wise friend told me he believed that Brains would've have known that, always. So it follows, your pet did, too.

Susie Cornfield, September 2009

If you have men who will exclude any of God's creatures from the shelter of compassion and pity, you will have men who deal likewise with their fellow men.

Not to hurt our humble brethren is our first duty to them, but to stop there is not enough. We have a higher mission — to be of service to them wherever they require it.

St Francis of Assisi

Hercules the mouse, and Brimble the dog

Averil Jarvis MBE,

founder and director, The Cinnamon Trust, Cornwall, UK

I have eight dogs and love them all for different reasons. They've taught me more about life and love than any human could. One of my dogs brought me this tiny baby wood mouse which I thought was dead and put in the dustbin. Later, I went to throw something away and saw the mouse open its mouth. I couldn't believe it. I took it out; it was blind in one eye and one front leg was dislocated badly. Using tweezers, I fed it oat flakes soaked in milk and, remarkably, it survived the night. There was only one name for this mouse – Hercules. The vet said nothing could be done for something so itsy bitsy so I brought Hercules home and someone I met on a walk made him a large oak house, with its own front door, dining room and bedroom.

The house had earth, straw and flowers on the floors and I used bottle tops for dishes. There were little wooden logs and loo roll tunnels to play in and only one tiny corner was ever soiled. Three weeks later, Hercules stood up, his bad leg mended. It was the best present on earth. Four days later, he looked at me with both eyes. I knew I'd witnessed a miracle.

I don't think Hercules would've survived in the wild, never having been taught what to do, but I never sought to tame him and he never showed any inclination to escape. He grew very fussy: not for him ordinary peas, they had to be *petit pois*. And if the choice of fare was not suitable, he threw his milk and water all over the place. I gave him seasonal berries, things I'd find in the garden or in the wild. He flourished and I adored him. I had him five years. Then one day I brought him an acorn I'd found in a hedgerow, which made him sick, and he died. The vet said it was paraquat, a highly poisonous weedkiller, and there was no antidote. To me, it was an absolute tragedy and you don't get over it, you just learn to come to terms with it. I went back to the hedgerow, which the poison spray had now turned brown, and thought what an indictment it was of what humans do.

But what's new? I was acquainted with an elderly lady who had an old Pyrenean mountain dog and a very nervous collie, both of whom she adored and took for walks three or four times a day. When she died, her body wasn't discovered for three days and the people who broke in found two terrified dogs who were immediately branded vicious and locked up in cold, dreadful kennels before being put down in not the kindest of ways. I was haunted by this event. I believed it to be utterly wrong, an absolute iniquity, that people should be forced to spend the end of their life without a beloved pet, and equally, that an old pet which had lost its owner should be put down or rehoused thoughtlessly.

The more I researched, the more I realised that people, even in their seventies, were anxious about having a pet, for fear of what might happen if they fell ill, became housebound, had to go into a home, or died. The solution was so simple but I didn't want to do it. I was happy, I was running a posh kennels, everything was going well for me, but, after 12 months of intense soul-searching and serious research, I sold up and established The Cinnamon Trust in 1985, named after my very special and much-beloved corgi.

I started with a small base, an Olivetti typewriter, a cardboard box and me. It was a hand-to-mouth existence and I had ghastly nightmares about how I was going to survive. But I'm stubborn, so today we have two sanctuaries, a new HQ building, 33 paid staff, and more than 7,500 volunteers nationwide, working individually or on a rota, looking after the pets of elderly or infirm people, sparing whatever time they can to walk a dog, feed a budgie, take a cat to the vet, or foster a pet when the owner is in hospital.

In this way, over the years, The Cinnamon Trust has helped elderly and terminally ill owners care for hundreds of thousands of animals, mostly cats and dogs and birds, but also a small pack of alpacas, and a homestead of 80-plus rabbits, each one known by name by their owner. We help animals continue to have a healthy, happy life, and we connect two people, an owner and a volunteer, as they sit over a cup of tea and talk about the pet they both care about. Sometimes, we ask an older bereaved owner to foster a pet who has lost its owner, which can help them both through a difficult time. And although we act only with the owner's consent (unless they're unconscious in hospital), we get referrals from doctors, social services, Macmillan nurses and the police. We're self-funded through donations, legacies and supporters' fundraising.

My faith, as well as many experiences I've had over the years, tell me that our animals are with us in an afterlife.

A strange thing happened not long after I started The Cinnamon Trust. The first dog to properly trial the first sanctuary was Brimble, a 14-year-old cocker spaniel, whose owner died. She'd obviously been much loved by him and she was a happy, gorgeous dog who readily woo-wooed with pleasure. At 18 she got pneumonia and although she recovered and was happy, she was frail and she'd stopped woo-wooing and pottered about, instead of going for long walks.

One day, I was taking a tray of dinners out to the dogs when Brimble started woo-wooing, which she hadn't done for weeks. I thought her tail would drop off, it was wagging so much. Her eyes and ears were alert, she was jumping up and down, and running alongside the fence. I felt a shiver go down my spine. She was greeting somebody I couldn't see. I knew I was going to lose her and she died the next day. But equally, I know from the pure delight emanating from that dog that she was greeting her dad who'd come to fetch her.

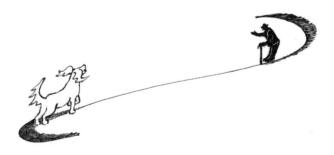

☆ The Trap

E. G. C. Beckwith

(from The Quill, a British Prisoner-of-War magazine)

"Snap!"
Goes the trap
Under my bed.
One feeble kick
(Which makes me rather sick)
And yet another mouse –
A tiny neighbour of my prison house –
Is dead,
And by my hand.
I'm sorry:
I did not understand,
It never struck me, when I went to get it
(That beastly trap), and baited it, and set it,
That you and I were somewhat on a par;
Nay, more, you were superior by far
In one respect, you funny little beast,
For you at least
Were free.
And who were we
To grudge such trifles as your fancy lit on?
Sampling your rations betwixt either mandible
You'd thought them dull, and stale (quite understandable

If hardly patriotic), and you hit on
This venture, to provide
A change for your diminutive inside.
Thoughtless, I only saw
You'd had a gnaw
At my provisions – chocolate, and cheese;
(My fault, of course for these
I should have put, for safety, in
A tin.)
I should indeed have thought of this before.
You are no more,
And no regrets can mend again, alack!
Your broken back.
How to atone for this untimely crime?
I'll think before I act another time;
And, when I take your carcase to its pyre
(The kitchen fire),
Old chap,
I'll add the trap.

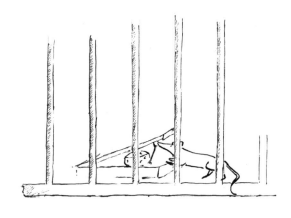

Requiem for Pluto

Anon

One large-sized collar hanging by the door
And one lead seldom used, now not needed any more.
One food bowl with Dog on it that you were using yesterday,
A lonely walk without you – but you were with me every
    moment of the way,
One newly-filled-in grave near the clothesline and the red May
    tree,
One heart very badly broken – and that belongs to me.

Smokey the cat, Jay the alligator, and the ants

Brian Fisher, Assistant Curator of Entomology,
California Academy of Sciences, San Francisco, USA

I grew up in Normal, Illinois, a small town in the Midwest of the USA surrounded by cornfields, and I guess I was always one of the Abnormals. There was me, my two sisters and my parents, who were both teachers. I collected any animal I could pick up – including dead ones, such as birds, which I kept in the freezer. I had salamanders, newts, frogs, turtles and fish, and a big grey Persian cat called Smokey who slept alongside me every night, after miaowing outside my window at 3.30 in the mornings to let her back in the house. She was with us for years and then, when I was about 14, she was run over and killed by a car. I remember the driver crying as she came up the garden path to tell us. We had a big burial in the backyard and I dug Smokey a large hole in the potato patch where the frosted ground was easier to work. I was devastated.

When I was five years old, my aunt bought me an alligator for 25 cents from an Arkansas pet shop. It was only a couple of inches long but over the years . . .

I called it Jay and, as we moved house a number of times, I built it bigger and bigger terrariums, basically dry habitats, with bigger and bigger ponds. When Jay was about ten years old he went missing in our house. I still wonder how a three foot long alligator with a ferocious appetite could go missing but he did. For seven days. My mother was in the shower and maybe a drop of water landed near him but the next she knew, she was sharing the shower with Jay. That's when she told me, quite loudly, that the alligator had to go.

First he went to my high school, living in a greenhouse behind the biology classroom. Whenever I wanted to skip out of class, I'd have someone come to the door and tell the teacher that Jay had escaped again. I contacted a zoo in Florida and they told me to duct-tape his jaws together and send him in the post. He arrived safe and sound and, as far as I'm aware, he's there to this day. But I have a feeling duct-taping alligators and mailing them is no longer an option.

Reading the *National Geographic*, I grew up thinking that my Midwest homeland was nowhere near as interesting as the tropics. So my ambition was to be a tropical researcher and explorer. I was a biology undergraduate at university in Iowa, and took a year off to research plants in the rainforest of an island in the Panama Canal.

I climbed the highest mountain, about 11,400 feet, to collect what I thought were rare if not unknown plants and when I brought them back, my tutor said I had nothing new. I was disappointed, to say the least. "What about the ants?" I asked, desperately. My tutor shrugged. "There's no way to identify them," he said. That was the defining moment in my life. When I knew what I wanted to do. I wanted to study ants. I was 20 and I began studying the relationship between plants and ants.

I discovered that an orchid, among other plants, builds a home inside itself to attract ants, which always protect their home. The ants also dump their garbage, which provides the plant with extra nutrients. Pretty soon, I'd dropped plants and concentrated on ants. Do you know there are 280 genera of ants, and some 20,000 species? That each ant has its own unique, beautiful face, and its own individual story? That an ant's worst enemy is another ant?

In my 20 years studying ants, I've had enormous fun and I've felt like an early explorer, like Darwin, discovering some 800 species of ant. I've also realized how out of touch  we've become with our environment. We may be literate but we're increasing bio-illiterate, ignorant of our environment and the wildlife within it. We may know a lot about Mars, but we know next to nothing about the insects on this planet. If we did know more, maybe we could improve on how we care for it and live in harmony with it.

I now have a beautiful, neurotic 18-month-old Border collie called Roxy, who's addicted inexplicably to asparagus. If I'm out of her sight for two seconds, she reacts on my return as though I've travelled to Borneo and back. She lives with my girlfriend and her children during the week and at weekends she has a totally different life as my house is in the woods. Of course, it's a very different and closer relationship with a pet than with an ant – but that said, I'd be very upset if some of the ants I've got at work died. Each ant has its own personality and behavior patterns you come to recognize and can predict, and in the wild the queen ants can live more than 40 years.

At the end of the day, I believe we have a brief moment on this earth and when our time is over we are reclaimed. As an American Indian said: "You think we own the land but we know the land owns us." So, yes, at some point, I'll get to be closer to my ants.

Alligator/Crocodile

Mary Ann Hoberman

The crocodile
Has a crooked smile.
The alligator's is straighter.

Or maybe it's the other way.
(With crocodiles it's hard to say.)

Perhaps the opposite is true.
(It's hard with alligators, too.)

But if I write what I just said,
The first way might be right instead.

And then again the second might
As easily be wrong or right.

Or right as wrong. Likewise the first.
In that case should they be reversed?

Chum the guinea pig,
and Beagle Bailey the dog

Paul Klusman, Engineer and Film Producer
of An Engineer's Guide to Cats *et al, Kansas, USA*

I come from a military family which moved around the US a fair bit, and my mom was big on indoor pets. There were always dogs, and strays. We did have a kitten for a few moments when I was seven or eight but because my sister Heidi's face swelled up very badly we had to find it another home. I was angry with her but at the same time I could see that she was also upset to have the kitten leave and I understood she could not help her allergic reaction.

One dog we had was Beagle Bailey, or BB. He was part of our family zoo of dogs, guinea pigs, Mom and Dad, and Heidi and me traveling over two days from North Dakota hundreds of miles south to Alabama. BB had eaten too much grass and my sister and I were each trying to push him on to the other when he threw up all over my sister's favorite dress. It was fantastic. There was uproar: my sister was crying, there was shouting . . . It's one of my most treasured childhood memories.

I didn't feel so upset when BB died. He'd been ill with a heart condition for some time so we knew the end was approaching when he went missing with his doggy playmate from next door and kids found his body a month later. What felt worse happened earlier.

My dad loved Beagle Bailey who'd run free daily in the

wooded areas around a park a few miles from where we were living in eastern Virginia. It became the norm that we'd leave him there, rootling for squirrels and rabbits, and return at sunset to collect him. Then one day he wasn't there. My dad got up very early the next morning and drove the car to the woods, slowly, slowly orbiting every road in the vicinity, when suddenly, in his rear-view mirror, he saw a little brown dog. BB! That made a big impression on me: that it was OK for a man to care deeply for a little animal.

My sister and I each had a guinea pig; hers was called Honeybear and mine was Chum and they lived together in a back room. Honeybear died early but expectedly from diabetes and it was only years later, when I was away from my family and lonely, that I suddenly realized what Chum must have felt like alone, for the first time in his life, with only five-minute daily visits from me. I think that's made me more aware in my dealings with my cats.

I lived without animals for a long time, partly because I lived close to my parents who always had pets. But five years ago when I moved to live and work 11 hours from home, before I got to know people and make friends, I did feel very lonely. That's when I came across this skinniest of cats, a Maine Coon, with a heartbreakingly sweet, friendly nature, which was hanging around the apartment complex. I reckoned she'd been abandoned and couldn't fend for herself so I began to feed her. Very soon Zoey, and her fleas, had moved in. I got rid of the fleas but not Zoey.

On that Tuesday night, when I didn't know anyone and I didn't want to go out on the town, I savored the unexpected discovery of having a companion. You say she was lucky to find me; I say I was the lucky one.

The following year, two little kittens began hanging around outside. I bitterly regret that one died while I was deciding what to do but I did bring in the other one, Ginger. A few years later came Oscar, who was filthy, walked with a limp and jumped into my car – at which point I guessed I was supposed to take care of him.

Because I want to be a film producer, I began making films about the cats, most famously *An Engineer's Guide to Cats*, which appears on YouTube and Yahoo, and has attracted some four million hits. I've had several hundred proposals of marriage and any number of messages from bereaved pet owners. One lady, whose pet was euthanased after it was wounded fatally by a neighbour, told me the film had restored her faith in human nature.

I never expected any of this and I'm glad that my little films help people through their bad and sad times, in much the same way my cats have helped me. Now I have to recognize that it won't be long before I have to say goodbye to Zoey, who has been diagnosed with diabetes. I can see that as well as my own sense of loss, my feline family dynamics will change, too. Ginger, sweet creature that she is, absolutely detests all other cats which live here or visit – excepting Zoey, whom she adores. How will she cope with her loss?

I'm an agnostic but without question, if I think I have a soul, then so does an animal. And to meet up again in an afterlife . . . well, that'd be marvellous, fantastic.

To love again

Anon

Oh what unhappy twist of fate
Has brought you homeless to my gate,
The gate where once another stood
To beg for shelter, warmth and food?

For from that day I ceased to be
The master of my destiny,
While she, with purr and velvet paw
Became within my house the law.

She scratched the furniture and shed
And claimed the middle of my bed,
She ruled in arrogance and pride
And broke my heart the day she died.

So if you really think, oh cat,
I'd willingly relive all that,
Because you come forlorn
and thin
Well, don't just stand there
– come on in!

Mabel the cat

David Crombie, gardener, south London, UK

We had a telephone call from a friend telling us of a cat which for the past six months had been living rough under a hedge. It seemed okay but with winter approaching and as our previous cat had passed on, they wondered . . .

We said yes, and they captured the cat and put her in their stables where she found a carpet tube to hide in. Although her rear end stuck out, she seemed quite comfortable so it was decided we'd leave her there for the time being. Our friends fed her, she got bigger and couldn't get into the tube any more so, in the October, we brought her home. We called her Mabel after the character in the Broadway musical, *Mack and Mabel*.

Mabel lived behind the settee for about four weeks, with her food and litter tray; she would not be tempted out. Then, for some reason, she moved upstairs into the wardrobe in our bedroom. So we put her box and food in there, and left the wardrobe door open. She'd had to have a lot of dental work and had only two incisors left. We'd wake up in the night to hear this prolonged, very noisy sucking coming from inside the wardrobe as she tried to eat. Eventually, she ventured into the kitchen for her food and to use the litter tray but, immediately after, she'd shoot back upstairs. It was very rare that she went outside of the house.

Mabel soon learnt to trust my wife, Sue, but it took a long time for her to learn to trust me. She'd cringe, as though she was waiting to be walloped. We felt so sorry for her; she must have been to hell and back. She was silent yet full of character. Everybody asked after her and some saw her watching them from a window and disappear the moment she saw them look back at her. She never made a sound, never miaowed, never made any demands whatsoever, but she was always purring. She must have felt content and safe. Perhaps she felt she'd found a sanctuary.

We'd had Mabel for two years and three months when she started putting on a lot of weight. Our vet diagnosed a cancerous tumour and said that she was old and probably had had enough. It made my blood run cold to hear that. I thought she'd been let down so many times, I felt desperate to explain to her what was going on and why. But I knew she had to be put to sleep then and there, because I wouldn't have the courage to go back.

The next few days were just appalling. For 48 hours, Sue and I made a conscious decision to talk as though she were there. We had her cremated and her ashes are inside a little box in a family field where our other cats are.

Sue didn't want the ashes scattered because she knew Mabel would feel safer if she were contained. In the same way, we still leave the wardrobe door open because somehow it feels right.

People say she was lucky to find us. I think the reverse is true. Mabel was a very fine cat.

Lonely House

Anon

No more cat tracks on the floor,
Muddy scratches on the door,
Puffs of hair upon the stairs,
Lacy fretwork on the chairs,

Indentations on my bed,
Markings where she laid her head,
Smudges on the window-pane
Showing where she watched in vain.

Haunts where she was wont to lay
Remind us that she is away.
My house is neater, that is true,
But, oh, how still and empty, too!

Daisy the rabbit

Charlotte Middleditch, student, Surrey, UK

I was seven and Victoria, my sister, was 10 when my mum took us to a pet shop in town. My sister saw a rabbit she wanted but I wanted it, too. I think I got her to change her mind by making a massive fuss. I wanted that particular rabbit because, as we stood by her cage, she jumped over to me, and this sounds stupid, but I felt we had a connection. So, Victoria got Dandelion and I got Daisy, a beautiful Dutch rabbit, half golden ginger, half white.

At first, I was really scared to pick her up because I didn't want to hurt her so when we got home I got Victoria to show me what to do. Then I went to check on Daisy every half-hour, and played with her and cuddled her.

The two rabbits didn't get on and they'd pull out each other's fur. Dandelion was sweet and gentle but Daisy was adventurous and had attitude. I liked her for that. When she was let out into the garden, she'd try to dig tunnels into our neighbour's garden and she tried to dig tunnels under her hutch. When we got close enough to catch her she'd stomp her two back feet to tell us to go away.

Dandelions were her favourite food and she liked carrots, grass, lettuce and cucumber. She'd eat anything, but not the packet food, the stuff that looks like muesli. She hated that.

I was really keen to teach her tricks – like jumping up the stairs, so that she could get into my room. I'm sure she knew it was my room and not anyone else's. But I got told off for that. She was allowed downstairs, but only in winter when it was cold.

to Charlotte's Room

I loved the way Skipper, my mum's godmother, and Daisy got on so well. Because of Skipper's health, she wasn't allowed to have an animal and Daisy would sit peacefully on her lap, without budging, for ages. I think that was nice for Skipper.

I had Daisy for five years and looked after her, fed her and cleaned out her cage until I had more to do at school. The day she died, Mum didn't tell me until she picked me up from school. Apparently, Mum'd gone out to feed Daisy and seen the top of the cage had been chewed away and all that was left of Daisy was her head. She'd been eaten by a fox. I ran out into the garden, crying. We all cried.

When Dandelion had died, we'd had a service and a grave, and played the song from *Titanic,* but for Daisy we didn't have a body, so Victoria, Mummy, Daddy and me stood in the garden and we remembered things about Daisy, like the time we brought her in for Christmas and she peed under the tree because she must've thought it was real. And the time we bought her a lead so we could take her for walks but it didn't fit because she was too fat.

It's three years since Daisy died and I still miss her. She was peaceful, patient and so cute. I used to come home from school and sit watching TV with her on my lap, cuddling her. I'd talk to her and she'd twitch her nose as though she heard what I was saying. I've got good friends and we talk about most things but I could talk to Daisy, tell her everything, and know she didn't tell anyone. I've got a photograph on my bookcase of us together, and I still think of her and still talk to her in my head.

☆

Epitaph on a Hare

William Cowper
1731–1800

Here lies, whom hound did ne'er pursue,
　Nor swifter greyhound follow,
Whose foot ne'er tainted morning dew,
Nor ear heard huntsman's hallo',

Old Tiney, surliest of his kind,
Who, nurs'd with tender care,
And to domestic bounds confin'd,
Was still a wild Jack-hare.

Though duly from my hand he took
His pittance ev'ry night,
He did it with a jealous look,
And, when he could, would bite.

His diet was of wheaten bread,
And milk, and oats, and straw,
Thistles, or lettuces instead,
With sand to scour his maw.

On twigs of hawthorn he regal'd,
On pippins' russet peel;
And, when his juicy salads fail'd,
Slic'd carrot please'd him well.

A Turkey carpet was his lawn,
Whereon he lov'd to bound,
To skip and gambol like a fawn,
And swing his rump around.

His frisking was at evening hours,
For then he lost his fear;
But most before approaching show'rs,
Or when a storm drew near.

Eight years and five round-rolling moons
He thus saw steal away,
Dozing out all his idle noons,
And ev'ry night at play.

I kept him for his humour' sake,
For he would oft beguile
My heart of thoughts that made it ache,
And force me to a smile.

But now, beneath this walnut-shade
He finds his long, last home,
And waits in snug concealment laid,
'Till gentler Puss shall come.

He, still more aged, feels the shocks
From which no care can save,
And, partner once of Tiney's box,
Must soon partake his grave.

Penny the hen, King the dog,
✩ and Josephine the bird

Stanley Smith, service veteran working with parrots in Serenity Park, Horticultural Therapy Program, Los Angeles, California, USA

I was born and raised on a farm in Missouri with two older sisters. We had cows and pigs that went to slaughter, and cats, dogs and chickens that were personal pets. We did love them all, but we learnt to let go of the ones that went to slaughter.

When I was seven or eight, I had my own hen, Penny, a Rhode Island, with a beautiful red tail, who'd sit on my arm. At night she'd roost in the doghouse and I propped up wood and bricks to protect her from weasels and the like. There wasn't much money around but I'd break into my meager savings and buy her food. I'd talk to her, and she'd cock her head, cluck and talk to me. She'd eat out of my hand; she wouldn't do that with anyone else.

I'd had her about three years when we left Missouri to move to California. I went to the provisions store where I bought her food, and sold her. I got a good price for her because she was fat and sassy and I wished her the best. To this day, and I'm in my 60s, I think of her.

When we moved, money was in short supply and there weren't any animals, and when I applied to join the Air Force I wanted to work with animals so I became a sentry dog handler, working nights in sensitive areas where weapons were kept. I remember my dog's registration, F157, and his name, O King of Troy. He was a good dog, gun-metal gray and white, with a small, pointed muzzle. He was small, about 75 lbs in weight and 27 inches tall, but he was very quick. He obeyed commands with the speed of a Jack Russell terrier. He wasn't an affectionate dog. He was kennelled with 16 other dogs and was trained to obey whoever took command of him. And although I might've liked to, it was the rule that I couldn't bring him home with me. He knew my family and was good with my two children who were about five and six at the time but, remember, he lived in kennels and only came out for turns of duty.

So how did I know he loved me? He'd nuzzle up to me. And he worked hard for me, to please me – that told me he did. But the time came when I got promotion to Kennel Master and I had to hand him on to someone else. I worked days now, so I fed him every day but it was against the rules to pct him. It was kinda tough on the old heartstrings but that's the way it was. I grew up on a farm and that teaches you how to cut loose. But emotions are always there, aren't they, in your mind, heart, body and soul?

I worked for years in hardware and got addicted to alcohol but now I've signed up for a year-long program. I reached a level to become eligible to do work therapy and I kinda lucked into this because an opening came up here in Serenity Park, working with abused, abandoned or injured parrots in a non-profit parrot refuge.

We've 31 birds here in an area about 25 square yards, with four big flight cages. Every one of the birds has had trouble in its life, like Matthew and I who work here, and you need a lot of patience and effort to win their trust. They're not like dogs that come when they're called; it's in their genes not to trust. It's a long

process and you know you've broken through when they react by preening and taking their eye off you, wandering about by your feet, or taking food from your hand. It's a great compliment.

Yes, I do have some favorites. I like the Amazons. They play about like silly kids who are bored. They are comical and they chatter, especially Josephine, the yellow-head who is very intelligent. Then there's Ruby and her sister, Magdalena, who came here tailless and now her tail has grown back, which means she no longer falls off her perch and she can fly.

I stay longer than my morning shift because there's more birds, more mess and more to do and because I want to. It's not for a pay check, it's a personal pleasure to work with these birds. They get cooked vegetables in the morning; later, fresh vegetables donated by the markets; and we hang fruit in the branches. The macaws and Amazons get peanuts and oatmeal mixed together. And there are feeders with seeds and nuts in. These birds are mostly too damaged to return to the wild so they're spoilt, and why not? Yes, I think I could move in here myself.

Would I miss any of the birds if one were to die? Yes, I would but, as I said, my farming background taught me to let go. You love them but you have to let go. You have to recognize that they are not in your life for ever. Perhaps it's for self-protection, to prevent getting hurt. But, then, I do believe in a heaven, an afterlife, where God's innocent creatures will be happy for ever. I hope I'll be there, too.

☆

If I can stop one heart from breaking

Emily Dickinson
1830–1886

If I can stop one heart from
    breaking,
I shall not live in vain;
If I can ease one life the aching,
Or cool one pain,
Or help one fainting robin
Unto his nest again,
I shall not live in vain.

Tammy the dog

Kay, Duchess of Hamilton,
chairwoman of Advocates for Animals, East Lothian, Scotland

I was a wreck after the death of my old dog, which I'd had for 17 years. My older dogs had died by this time and the grief was awful. During that time I was neither reasonable nor sensible. Tammy was a black Staffordshire with great melting eyes and I'd had her from the day she was born; her mother, Nikki, was one of my three Staffies. Nikki was worn out after producing her litter and her sister, Kerri, brought up Tammy and tried to teach her the rough and tumble of life but Tammy would just roll over on her back and almost laugh; fighting wasn't in her nature. I loved Tammy and Tammy loved me, and that was it. Even food came second to me; if I were in a hurry, she'd leave her bowl rather than miss coming out with me.

I'd been ill and I collapsed on the beach near our home. I must've been unconscious for a few minutes and when I came round, Tammy was there, sitting, waiting and licking me. I know she would never have left me. And when the minister's wife was out for a walk and fell, breaking her leg, it was their rescue Staffie who walked with her the half-mile to the main road, side by side, step by step of the way.

Over the years, I must've rescued and re-homed hundreds and hundreds of Staffies (it's how I met my husband, when he came to get a dog for one of his children) and you wouldn't believe the way people treat them. The dogs come in bruised, ribs smashed, legs broken, faces slashed and yet, with love, they become loyal and loving pets. But I don't think they forget what happened to them: Clio came to us in a real mess and took several years to settle down, but if ever she saw an odd boot "suddenly" appear in the hall, she'd scream. Another dog, totally settled after a careless upbringing, would not stop barking when one day a tall red-haired man appeared on the doorstep. I despair that Staffies now have such a bad name; it's totally undeserved. It's all down to rotten, irresponsible breeders and owners.

I think I get my love of Staffies from my father who said that they were like good men: independent, kind, gentle and wonderful with children but could take good care of themselves in a fight.

I grew up in a nice rented two-room tenement in the harbour area of Aberdeen and my father was always bringing home waifs and strays, people he felt were down on their luck, and damaged pigeons, injured rabbits, cats or kittens, which would've been drowned otherwise. My parents included other children in our fun, and we were often a jolly little disparate bunch on the beach, laughing, playing and picnicking.

I was 16 when I got Peter, my first and very own Staffie. I'd heard of a litter of puppies whose mother had been killed in a car accident. The accountant in the office where I worked kindly lent me the money to buy a pup and a friend took me to collect it and bring it home. When my mother saw it, she said "That's not staying in the house", before ordering me to get hot water to clean him up and a blanket for him to sleep on. Peter stayed and, in no time, became mother's dog – although if you came into the room when Peter had his head on her lap, she'd get embarrassed

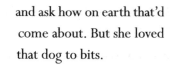

and ask how on earth that'd come about. But she loved that dog to bits.

Yes, I've rescued turkeys, too. They're delightful creatures; they enjoy being stroked and petted and, like us, they're vegetarians. One year, we filmed my first turkey, Ankora, sitting on my knee as we had a very nice veggie Xmas meal. When one of the last two had to be put down, the other saw what was going on. I carried the dead bird outside and Drew buried her. When I came back in the other turkey, the dead one's friend, pecked me good and proper. Understandably, she was upset. Later that day, our housekeeper found her surrounded by the hens, which normally stayed apart in separate sheds. I also remember when all the other dogs had died, Tammy would never walk the path they'd trodden; we had to take a different route always. I think we forget that animals have these feelings.

Actually, I can't understand some people's attitude towards animals. Once, on a visit to France, we saw a crowd of people laughing and joking as they watched a flock of geese being force-fed through tubes stuck down their throats (for *foie gras*); the look of fear and pain on the faces of these creatures was dreadful to behold. How can one human being see it as distress and others have no comprehension or compassion?

My husband stopped all game shooting on the estate in the 1970s and a friend of ours has trained his Labrador not to chase rabbits. My husband and I think the idea of killing animals for fun is utterly barbaric. There are also immensely cruel and unnecessary acts: I work with Advocates for Animals, trying to get banned in Scotland the snares used on many estates. Snaring is indiscriminate, catching badgers and dogs, and cats and, on one occasion, a sea otter. It was an icy night and she slipped into the undergrowth. We never found her; she must have died a most dreadful death.

I don't know about an afterlife but I hope I end up with my family and friends, and that includes my animals. I believe heaven and hell are made here on earth and the afterlife will probably be a peaceful state – knowing and feeling rather than seeing those loved ones around.

☆

HE IS VERY imprudent a dog;
he never makes it his business to inquire
whether you are in the right or the wrong,
never asks whether you are rich or poor,
silly or wise, sinner or saint.
You are his pal. That is enough for him…

Jerome K. Jerome 1859–1927

☆

When I got my new dog

Anon

I asked for strength that I might rear her perfectly;
I was given weakness that I might feed her more treats.

I asked for good health that I might rest easy;
I was given a "special needs" dog that I might know nurturing.

I asked for an obedient dog that I might feel proud;
I was given stubbornness that I might feel humble.

I asked for compliance that I might feel masterful;
I was given a clown that I might laugh.

I asked for a companion that I might not feel lonely;
I was given a best friend that I would feel loved.

I got nothing I asked for,
But everything I needed.

Crocus the cat, and two strays,
☆   a dog and a goat

Brigitte Bardot, animal rights campaigner, Provence, France

I live in Provence in the French Midi – it's here that I've accumulated all my animals, around 50. Horses, donkeys, ponies, goats, sheep, pigs, geese, hens, ducks and, of course, cats and dogs. During the Second World War I lived in a flat in Paris, where I spent my childhood. It wasn't possible to have an animal there, but later on we had a cat named Crocus who made me so happy while I was growing up. Much later on my parents had a little black cocker spaniel called Youki but by then I had more or less left home.

When I was making films I used to rescue all the stray animals and bring them back to the hotel. This got me into trouble one time when I brought back a little goat to a four-star hotel during the filming of my last film, *Colinot Trousse Chemise*. The little goat slept in my bed with the little dog that I'd brought back as well, and I told the hotel manager to get lost. Both animals stayed with me until their deaths, many years later.

I've always loved animals since I was a small child. I was born with this passion and was frustrated at not being able to have any when I was little. As soon as I stopped living with my parents I had animals, which I acquired from all over the place. Animals are part of the natural order of things. They share with us a planet where they are denied the right to live as their territory is destroyed. They're slaughtered for money and held hostage. It's

dreadful to destroy them with such violence and to use such force against them when they're so vulnerable. It's inexcusable to put them through the suffering of animal testing, slaughterhouses, fur farms, bullfights.

Now I spend my days with my 50 animals. I love them unconditionally. Most have been rescued from slaughter or from being put down. They've all got names – my mare Melodie; my pony Ficelle; my little donkey Bonhomme; my pigs Marcel, Rosalie, Valentin, Rillette; my goats Babybouc, Carmen, Patchoulie. There are the six dogs – Toutsie, Alba, Loupiotte, Parafine, Olga, and the male one, Roudoudou – the geese, and more than 25 cats.

For me, paradise would be to be reunited with all my animals, all the ones I've loved so much and who took a bit of me with them when they died. Otherwise, if it means meeting up with all this humanity, from which I've fled, I'd rather be in hell.

Song of the Battery Hen

Edwin Brock

1927–1997

We can't grumble about accommodation:
we have a new concrete floor that's
always dry, four walls that are
painted white, and a sheet-iron roof
the rain drums on. A fan blows warm air
beneath our feet to disperse the smell
of chicken shit and, on dull days,
fluorescent lighting sees us.

You can tell me: if you come by
the north door, I am in the twelfth pen
on the left-hand side of the third row
from the floor; and in that pen
I am usually the middle one of three.
But, even without directions, you'd
discover me. I have the same orange-
red comb, yellow beak and auburn
feathers, but as the door opens and you
hear above the electric fan a kind of
one-word wail, I am the one
who sounds loudest in my head.

Listen. Outside this house there's an
orchard with small moss-green apple
trees; beyond that, two fields of
cabbages; then, on the far side of
the road, a broiler house. Listen:
one cockerel grows out of there, as
tall and proud as the first hour of sun.
Sometimes I stop cackling with the others
to listen, and wonder if he hears me.

The next time you come here, look for me.
Notice the way I sound inside my head.
God made us all quite differently,
and blessed us with this expensive home.

Stray goat

Elizabeth Montagu

1720–1800

from a letter to the Duchess of Portland, 17th December, 1738

I heard a very ridiculous story a few days ago: Mr Page, brother to Sir Gregory, going to visit Mr Edward Walpole, a tame goat which was in the street followed him unperceived when he got out of the coach into the house. Mr Walpole's servant, thinking the goat came out of Mr Page's coach, carried it into the room to Mr Walpole, who thought it a little odd Mr Page should bring such a visitor, as Mr Page no less admired his choice of so savoury a companion; but civility, a great disguiser of sentiments, prevented their declaring their opinions, and the goat, no respecter of persons or furniture, began to rub himself against the frame of a chair which was carved and gilt, and the chair, which was fit for a Christian, but unable to bear the shock of a beast, fell almost to pieces. Mr Walpole thought Mr Page very indulgent to his dear crony the goat, and wondering he took no notice of the damage, said he fancied tame goats did a great deal of harm, to which the other said he believed so too: after much free and easy behaviour of the goat, to the great detriment of the furniture, they came to an explanation, and Mr Goat was turned downstairs . . .

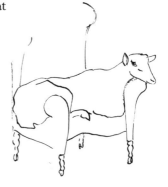

Little Sue and Naru,
the orang-utans

Trevor Knight OBE, *former head librarian, Berkshire,* UK

I was born and brought up in West Bromwich in the west Midlands. My father worked in the steel mills and my mother stayed at home, caring for me and my sister who's 13 years my senior. We weren't particularly animal people, but there was always a dog in our house. One was Brumus, a lovely-natured beast, a black mongrel, and I remember him best because when I was a toddler I tripped over him and fell down the stairs.

Since she married my sister has always had cats, to which I'm not partial because they bring me out in huge water blisters, but she did have a lovely gentle marmalade creature who was called Wilkins, after the hero of a children's book. He was a chilled-out being. Unlike most cats I've met, Wilkins did not give you the evil eye that says, *I'll get you*.

After I'd qualified as a librarian I had three or four jobs around the country where I never stayed long enough to even consider having an animal. But in Somerset, living in a flat on a working farm, I did have my eyes opened as to how a different life can shape people's opinions. I saw a field of dead lambs that'd been killed by a fox. It was an awful sight and for the farmer it meant a large part of his livelihood had been wiped out. I understood better why people support fox hunting.

My work and my love of travel really precluded having an animal but I have always had a love of orang-utans. Why? As well as being beautiful, as well as looking desperately sad even when they're doing something they enjoy, they are absolutely fascinating creatures. They don't skitter about as do monkeys, they're purposeful and reflective. And there are many parallels with man, one being they stay with their mother for a long time, six to eight years, because they need to: they don't know things instinctively, they have to learn them.

I watch any programme on TV about orang-utans and I visit them in zoos or parks when we've been abroad. In Florida I watched one orang-utan pick the individual leaves off a lettuce and wash each one in the river before eating it. And I saw a David Attenborough programme in which after a few days' filming, he and his crew discovered their canoe had been commandeered. A baby orang-utan sat at the prow while the mother was using the paddles to row the boat along the river.

Yes, I can watch them for hours, and have, which is how I became an adoptive parent to Little Sue and Naru.

As I said, I like my holidays but jungles and rainforests are just not my thing. That said, four years ago, because of the chance to see orang-utans, I went to Borneo, to the Sepilok Rehabilation Centre, 43 sq. km of protected land on the edge of a forest reserve, founded in 1964 to rehabilitate orphan orang-utans.

The rainforest was pretty horrific for me, leeches and insects and all that kind of stuff, but on the third day in the late afternoon, we were very fortunate: the ranger called us to fetch our binoculars. It's a pastime requiring patience, watching orang-utans, and we watched for three or four hours as an orang-utan built his bed for the night in the top of a tree in the dense canopy of the forest.

If you get to Sepilok at a certain time in the morning you can watch the orang-utans come out of the forest and eat on the wooden platform. These are creatures orphaned most often by loggers who kill their mothers. Sometimes people find them and bring them in to the centre. They're put into a nursery, where they wear nappies until they're trained to use special dung areas.

It doesn't happen now but there was a time when the orang-utan babies came into contact with people, against whom they have no natural immunity. Which was how Little Sue got ill. She caught a chill and died, as did a few other babies. I was very sad. You get an adoption certificate, lovely newsletters and pictures twice a year. Little Sue had been doing so well, I felt like a godparent watching over her from afar, and then came this letter, albeit a very nicely written letter, telling me that she'd died. And I did get very upset.

I was asked if I'd like to adopt another. And so now I'm godfather to Naru, who arrived at the centre three years ago weighing 1.6 kilos and who now, at four years old, weighs 14 kilos. He's a very handsome lad, just changing from baby to adolescent, and my latest letter tells me that he's just learning to stand up for himself against a bully.

Within a few years hopefully he'll be released, in a gradual process, back into the wild. That'll be brilliant. I'll be absolutely delighted if he makes it, if he can become independent and lead the life of a normal wild animal, growing possibly to 175 cm and weighing 118 kg.

I know some people might say that this is an easy way to have an animal, and I'd agree. I don't have to do any mopping up. I'm not tied down in any way. But it doesn't stop me grieving for the loss of Little Sue at such a young age. And hopefully people such as me, who support adoptive animal charities, spread the word in the West about how the demands of our greedy lifestyle destroy the environment in other countries, as well as beautiful creatures such as Little Sue.

✩

UNTIL ONE HAS
loved an animal,
a part of one's soul
remains unawakened.
Anatole France
1844–1924

✩

Reflections

Virginia McKenna

Inside the palm, beneath the searching fingers
The skin is pink and wrinkled.
Just like mine.

Eyes behind the mesh behind the glass
Look into my eyes.
Same thoughts. I know.

Sad, mad monkey
In that twilight box.
Reflected in the glass,
Dim outline in that silent, sordid world
I see myself, and you beyond.
Trapped. Forever.
In my memory.

What is your question?
Why?
Mine is the same.

Jack the bird, and Barley the dog

Mark Habben,

team leader, Animal Activities Department, London Zoo, UK

Animals have been a life-long passion. When I was three or four I was turning over stones for worms, and looking for caterpillars, spiders and frogs. My father and both grandfathers were very encouraging. I think my mother's attitude is best described as extremely tolerant, especially when I was 11 and breeding snakes and the cat dislodged the lid from a glass cabinet, freeing 22 baby North American garter snakes into the house which we were still finding weeks later.

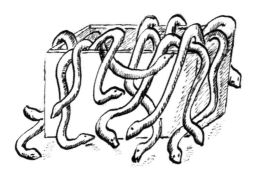

After a school-trip to London Zoo, I kept nagging my parents to take me back again and again, and once I said how much I wanted to live in the Keeper's Lodge, little knowing that a few years on, I'd be doing just that. I love London Zoo, not only for its history, being the first zoo in the world, but for its conservation and educational work. I got a job at the Zoo after doing a degree in animal biology and then took a six-month break to lead a group of volunteers researching wildlife in the Amazon, returning to the Zoo in this managerial position, working out programmes which encourage specific, natural behaviours in animals such as kangaroos and owls, meerkats and eagles, while providing the public with a view of their life.

We're encouraged not to get too attached to an animal but, that said, it's difficult not to form an attachment to some. I worked for six years with a kookaburra called Jack. I went into his cage every day to feed him, to exercise and fly him, or simply to see him. He was a beautiful bird, personable, feisty but gentle, and fun. He was also a natural performer. We'd throw food into the air above the heads of an audience of 700 and he'd fly up and catch it before it landed, often taking in a few insects along the way. He never missed. He had a phobia about helicopters, which in London is a bit of a problem. He'd fly off and huddle somewhere until the helicopter's noise was far away and he'd come down only when we shook his rubber snake. He'd swoop down, grab hold of it and give it a thorough shaking, just as kookaburras do with real snakes in the wild, but really for longer than was absolutely necessary.

One day I was in early and thought it odd that I hadn't heard Jack's usual call, to which I'd always respond, so I went to check him out. He was sitting on the floor, surrounded in blood and feathers, and I realised one of his wings was damaged. I rushed to get the vet who examined him and said he'd never fly again and that the kindest thing was to euthanase him. I lifted him up, took him into the operating theatre and held him until he stopped breathing. It was heartbreaking and I can't say that I didn't shed a tear.

Kookaburras are very territorial and we found out later that Jack's injury had been caused by a fox which he'd seen off before, but not this time. For weeks afterwards, the staff were very subdued: the cage was empty and Jack left a void. But I like to remember him as he was – a happy bird.

At home, perhaps the best animals to get close to are dogs. They are absolutely fantastic; they'd do anything for you, no matter who or what you are. I had my first dog when I was 13 or 14 and I was so ecstatic when she arrived that I didn't want to go to school.

Barley was a stunningly beautiful cross Border collie and Labrador, like a little white fox when she was a pup. She was a real head turner and I called every friend I could think of to come and take a look at her. She was intelligent and obedient; she never needed to be on a lead. And she was always there with a comforting paw, seeming to know your mood or if you'd had a bad day.

She was also a lady. I used to take her on walks and on bird-watching trips where she'd sit quietly beside me, as she did with my dad when he took her to the pub. The only thing she hated was water. If we were out on a walk and it started to rain, that was one thing, but if we tried to set off when it was raining, she'd sit on the doorstep and wouldn't budge. She hated getting her paws wet. She avoided puddles. It was almost as if she expected us to lay down our coats on them for her. Bless her.

Barley was my constant companion for more than a decade and then last year, the night after Guy Fawkes, she did something she never did: she jumped on to the sofa and when my dad ordered her off, she jumped back up again. The next day my mum found her dead in the kitchen. We never did find out the specific cause of Barley's death but I think it's safe to say that it was a result of the noise of the fireworks, which she hated.

I felt physically sick when my mum told me the news, an emotional wreck. Barley was irreplaceable. The next day I went out on one of the walks we used to do together and carved Barley's name and date of birth on an oak tree we used to pass. I still do the walk. I like to check her name's still there. We lost her too young and I wanted to immortalise her.

Is there an after-life? Who's to say? If there is, it has to be inclusive of animals.

The Dead Sparrow

William Cartwright

1611–1643

Tell me not of joy; there's none,
  Now my little Sparrow's gone:
He, just as you,
Would try and woo,
He would chirp and flatter me;
He would hang the wing awhile –
Till at length he saw me smile
Lord, how sullen he would be!

He would catch a crumb, and then
Sporting, let it go agen;
He from my lip
Would moisture sip;
He would from my trencher feed;
Then would hop, and then would run,
And cry *Philip* when he'd done.
O! whose heart can choose but bleed?

O how eager would he fight,
And ne'er hurt, though he did bite.
No morn did pass,
But on my glass
He would sit, and mark and do
What I did – now ruffle all
His feathers o'er, now let 'em fall;
And then straightaway sleek them too.

Whence will Cupid get his darts
Feathered now to pierce our hearts?
A wound he may
Not, Love, convey,
Now this faithful bird is gone;
O let mournful turtles join
With loving red-breasts, and combine
To sing dirges o'er his stone!

Dog's Death

John Updike

1932–2009

She must have been kicked unseen or brushed by a car.
Too young to know much, she was beginning to learn
To use the newspapers spread on the kitchen floor
And to win, wetting there, the words, "Good dog! Good dog!"

We thought her shy malaise was a shot reaction.
The autopsy disclosed a rupture in her liver.
As we teased her with play, blood was filling her skin
And her heart was learning to lie down forever.

Monday morning, as the children were noisily fed
And sent to school, she crawled beneath the youngest's bed.
We found her twisted and limp but still alive.
In the car to the vet's, on my lap, she tried

To bite my hand and died. I stroked her warm fur
And my wife called in a voice imperious with tears.
Though surrounded by love that would have upheld her,
Nevertheless she sank and, stiffening, disappeared.

Back home, we found that in the night her frame,
Drawing near to dissolution, had endured the shame
Of diarrhoea and had dragged across the floor
To a newspaper carelessly left there. *Good dog.*

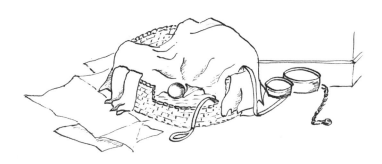

Fortnum, Hero *et al*, the dogs

☆

Jilly Cooper, writer, broadcaster and media star, Gloucestershire, UK

✿

I remember Jamie, our Scottie dog, who had to be put down when I was four years old and my mother crying as if her heart were breaking. She'd lost relations and friends but she cried more over that little dog. Her face was carved up by grief and I remember feeling embarrassed as well as wondering how to comfort her. There was Penny, a Sealyham, Freckles, a springer spaniel, and Simmie, a golden retriever, who was a terrible wanderer. We got a call one day from the local cinema to say that he'd been shaking hands with the projectionist for the last half-hour and could we come and get him so that they could start the film.

Later, there was Fortnum, a mongrel, who had sex with every bitch he encountered and fought every dog he met. I loved him passionately but I had to have him put down after he killed a dog. It was dreadful, absolutely dreadful. In his early life, he'd had to be cut down from a cross; a gang of louts had tried to crucify him. The next owner who took him in found that he cried whenever she left him. She was on her way to take him to Battersea Dogs and Cats Home when I met her. I took him in then and there. We had him about six years.

Barbara was an offspring of one of his sprees. I remember

she had a very vulgar curly tail which, after we moved to the country, was stung by a wasp and fell into a long, curved patrician lurcher's tail. There was also Mabel, Bessie and Hero, who was my heroine. She was beautiful, elegant and charming, although she bit Leo most mornings (well, he does have heavy feet), and actually bit quite a lot of other people. But it was fear-biting, because she was very, very shy and came to me as a puppy when she'd just lie in my arms, utterly helpless.

Perhaps because I couldn't have children, although we have two wonderful adopted children, my dogs have all been particularly special. And now they've gone, there are pictures of them everywhere in the house. In fact, I can't see myself in the bathroom mirror any more because of the pictures.

All of them, except Fortnum, who died in Putney, are in a graveyard by the tennis court. And they've all got their own epitaphs. Every time one of our animals dies, I sit down almost immediately and chronicle its life, habits and endearing tricks and its last hours, so I have about ten pages on each. I recommend it as a way of preserving memories, which might otherwise be lost.

Hero died at the end of last year and this is the first time in 35 years that I've been without a dog. It's ghastly. The only flipside

is that, thriving on new attention, our five cats have blossomed. With five of them, I have to have a stroking rota in case they get jealous. There is more room on the bed and Leo doesn't get bitten when he reaches out for me in the middle of the night, but it feels so empty when you go for a walk without a dog.

There's so much anti-dog attitude about nowadays, fines here and there in parks and outside people's homes, but I think you get colossal amounts of uncritical love from a dog, as well as fun, merriment, cuddles and endless companionship. And I've made friends with people I've met walking the dogs, friends now of 30 years' standing.

My dogs have seen me through so many difficult times and they've also helped me really learn about and appreciate wildlife, trees and flowers I observe on my walks. While I was taking them out late at night, I also taught myself the stars.

A kind friend wants to give me a lurcher pup for Christmas, but I'm trying to be strong and wait till the summer. I've got a huge book coming out and with all the publicity running up to publication and a three-week book tour after that, it wouldn't be fair on a new dog to keep leaving it when it'd only just arrived. I am actually hoping to get two dogs so they can be companions, and when one dies you don't have an utterly dog-less house, as I have now.

I like the idea that when you die and, hopefully, reach heaven, all your animals come bounding over a sunlit lawn to greet you. Do I believe they're there in an after-life? Yes, yes, of course. You have to believe that, don't you? It's just too awful to think one won't see one's dogs again.

Jilly Cooper's book Animals in War *was written to accompany the first* Animals in War *exhibition at the Imperial War Museum in 1983, and all royalties from it go to the Animals in War Memorial Fund. The memorial is in Park Lane, London.*

An Epitaph

Lord Byron
1788–1824

Near this spot
 Are deposited the remains of one
Who possessed beauty without vanity,
Strength without insolence,
Courage without ferocity,
And all the virtues of man without his vices.

This praise, which would be unmeaning flattery
If inscribed over human ashes,
Is but a just tribute to the memory of
Boatswain, a dog.

Inscription on a monument at Newstead Abbey

Tess and Cica, the dogs

General Sir Richard Dannatt,
Chief of General Staff 2006–2009, London, UK

Much to the dismay of my children, I had to admit to them I was born and brought up in a "cat" household. I didn't like dogs until I was in my early twenties and met a Jack Russell terrier, named Snap, who belonged to a university friend. It transpired that I was the first potential boyfriend she'd had who Snap liked. That did it: I was converted to dogs. And I married my girlfriend soon after we graduated from Durham.

Throughout our 32 years of marriage, we've always had dogs, between one and five – Labradors, terriers, spaniels. All different characters. The first dog we had was when I was serving in Berlin. Cica was an elderly, doddery Labrador, who'd had already six postings to the city. He was inclined to wander out of our house in the barracks and there were times when I had to call the guards at the gate to apprehend and arrest him if they saw him strolling by, and I'd pick him up from the cells.

I remember we were at a lunch party and the host's dog, a lively Weimaraner, kept jumping over the fence into a neighbour's garden. Cica decided to follow suit and got himself caught on the jagged fencing. He nearly died, surviving only after expensive treatment at the vet. Animals are good at requiring expensive vet treatment.

When we left Berlin Cica went to live with an American family who adored him and took him back to the States, as their quarantine laws at that time were more lenient than ours, where he ended his days happily on French fries and ice cream.

When I was commanding a brigade in Bosnia in 1995/6 we adopted two mutts – one we named Black Dog, the other White Fang. We were overseeing the Dayton Peace Plan, involving the opening of two routes into the Serb part of Bosnia. We named the two crossing points in honour of those two dogs. Sadly, White Fang shoved off after a few weeks but Black Dog went on to have nine puppies all of which were "bagged" by army personnel. When I said it was time for the puppies to go (as in, go to their new owners), someone misunderstood and took the puppies to be sold at market. When she heard, the officer-in-charge raced off in a Land Rover to get them back. She managed to retrieve two. But I think it shows the great and inherent sentimentality of the great British Army.

I do a fair bit of game shooting and so have a gun dog, either a black or a yellow Labrador. I've had good dogs and less good dogs but Tess was one of the best. She came from the home of a Norfolk gamekeeper who found she didn't fit in with his spaniels. She was 18 months old, no longer a puppy, which meant less mud and mess round the house, which pleased my wife.

Our three sons and daughter loved Tess, we all did, but she wasn't terribly disciplined. However, we struck up a good relationship: I didn't trust her and she didn't expect to be trusted. So, on shoots, I kept her on a lead, pegged to the ground, releasing her only to fetch birds. Then she was in her element. She had a good nose and a soft mouth, and she was determined. Invariably, she'd quickly pick up my birds, and find lost ones – the longer the hunt the better!

My parents-in-law lived five miles from our family home and once they took in all our dogs while we were away on holiday. On our return home early in the morning we walked in to find Tess in her basket. She'd wandered out of my in-laws' house and walked the five miles home. Our lodger had got home late to find her on the doorstep, waiting patiently to be let in. And there she was, waiting for us. Amazing creature. All our dogs technically belong to one or other of the children – Tess belonged to Tom, our eldest son. On one occasion they went to a fancy-dress party together, Tess dressed in a white collar as the vicar. They won first prize!

Towards the end of her life, she had to have an operation to remove a lump the size of a small rugby ball. There she was, stitched up, swathed in bandages, and fully sedated in her basket. The next we knew she'd got up, gone out down to the river by our house – for a swim. The first we knew of it was her bedraggled figure, bandages covered in mud, returning home triumphant.

Yes, she was a go-for-it, free spirit of a dog.

I was serving in Kosovo in summer 1999, due to return home in August, when my wife said Tess's health was fading and that my first job on my return home must be to take her to the vet to be put down. I was looking forward to coming home but I didn't want to take my much-loved dog to the vet for the deed to be done. I arrived home with a heavy heart only to find that Sgt Crighton, who'd been with me then for ten years, keeping me in order, had overseen the deed. I was, and remain, immensely grateful to him.

We don't go down the path of shrines and things. We're harder nosed. But we do like to think that when we die we'll find all our dogs there. It might be a childish notion but if heaven is a place to look forward to, it must be that people you've loved will be there together with all the animals you've loved. I think Tess will be there – and Cica, and . . .

✧

If a dog be well remembered
✧

Ben Hur Lampman ✧

published in The Oregonian, Portland, USA, 11 September 1925

We are thinking now of a dog, whose coat was flame in the sunshine and who, so far as we are aware, never entertained a mean or an unworthy thought. This dog is buried beneath a cherry tree, under four feet of garden loam, and at its proper season the cherry strews petals on the lawn of his grave. Beneath a cherry tree or an apple or any flowering shrub of the garden is an excellent place to bury a good dog. Beneath such trees, such shrubs, he slept in the drowsy summer or gnawed at a flavorous bone or lifted head to challenge some strange intruder. These are good places, in life or in death.

Yet it is small matter. For if a dog be well remembered, if sometimes he leaps through your dreams actual as in life, eyes kindling, laughing, begging, it matters not at all where the dog sleeps. On a hill where the wind is unrebuked and the trees roaring, or beside a stream he knew in puppyhood, or somewhere in the flatness of a pastureland where most exhilarating cattle graze. It is all one to the dog, and all one to you, and nothing is gained and nothing is lost – if memory lives.

But there is one best place to bury a dog. If you bury him in this spot, he will come to you when you call – come to you over the grim, dim frontiers of death, and down the well-remembered path, and to your side again. And though you call a dozen living dogs to heel they shall not growl at him, nor resent his coming, for he belongs there. People may scoff at you, who see no lightest blade of grass bent by his footfall, who hear no whimper, people who may never really have had a dog. Smile at them, for you shall know something that is hidden from them, and which is well worth knowing.

The one best place to bury a dog is in the heart of his master.

Rover the fish

Jonathan Stone, accountant, south London, UK

Aside from my brother, I lived an animal-free life until my mid-thirties when I decided I wanted some fish. I did the research and got a tank, 4ft by 2ft 6in., a pump, some rocks and underwater toys and then a goldfish I called Fido and a blue koi carp, about the length of a pencil, which I called Rover.

Rover and Fido were a pleasure to have around. They were beautiful to look at and were very low maintenance. They were peaceful; they didn't answer back. They didn't complain about my music, didn't mind if I came home late and, unlike me, weren't faddish about their food.

I lost Fido after 18 months and I buried him in the garden. For years it was just me and Rover. Then I got burgled. Sometimes I wonder if the shock of it all killed Rover. He went off his food, started swimming backwards and began to look poorly. So one day I put him into a large, 550-gram jar, punched holes in the lid, and very slowly drove him to the vet.

The surgery was full of cats and dogs and rabbits and I think a fish was the last thing the vet was expecting. He opened the jar and began pouring out the water but, instead of landing in a tiny metal container, Rover slithered all round the table before either of us could get hold of him. Then the vet put a two-inch syringe into his flesh, behind his gill, and I took him home and put him back in his tank. I kept an eye on him as I had my supper. He did not look in the best of health. The next morning I found him floating on top of the water.

I put him in a box and buried him, near Fido, at the bottom of the garden. I was upset. We'd been together, man and fish, for a good few years. I'd have liked to have given him a Viking funeral, put him in a small boat at sunset and pushed him out to sea, but that kind of thing isn't possible in south London.

I had a few other fish – Metro, Maestro and Mini – but not one matched up to Rover.

☆

If God had wanted a Gerbil
☆

Anon   ☆

If God had wanted a gerbil
He should have saved up like me
And gone to the pet shop and bought one
That's doing things properly.

If God had wanted a gerbil
Then I think it awfully mean
To have made me drop mine and kill it
When I fed it and kept it so clean.

If God had wanted a gerbil

He should have taken its cage and straw

No, I won't have another gerbil

Just in case God wants some more.

☆

Benson the fish, and Billy the dog

☆

Tony Bridgefoot, proprietor, Bluebell Lakes,
Peterborough, Cambridgeshire, UK

I was born and brought up in a village called Upwell in Norfolk. Fen country, barren, bleak, rivers and ditches, and great big skies. You can see the rain clouds coming from miles away. I love it. Never have got used to hills, if I'm honest. I'm a middle child, between two brothers and two sisters. My father met my mother when he was serving as a soldier in Germany during the Second World War and she came to England in 1946 to be married.

My father was a general factory worker and my mother was a dressmaker. It wasn't that they didn't like animals, but we didn't have pets. But when I came to marry and settle down, I decided having a pet was for me. And luckily, it was the same for my wife, Lynn. And we've had dogs ever since. Our first dog was a black Labrador which we called Spot – after the little dog in the TV children's programme, *The Woodentops*, which I watched every week as a child and loved.

Was Spot special? Yes, indeed. But all your animals become special, don't they? They all have their own special traits.

We had a small Cairn terrier, Whisky, for 14 years, like Spot. He was a proper character, a stubborn little fellow. And then we had two Cairns, Billy and Alf. Billy died 11 months ago and I'm still heartbroken. Right from the start, he was my dog. He attached himself to me, without me doing anything, without me having to try to be anything than who I am. I liked that. He'd sit with me, walk with me, and enjoy a playtime of rough and tumble. He was altogether happy simply to be in my company.

Alf was Lynn's dog. We thought of him as behaving like a spoilt only child. He does things when he likes and he doesn't "do" company. He mourned for his brother Billy for about six months, losing interest in anything and everything, and I believe he still thinks of him from time to time. He's more sociable now and when we go walking by the lake, near to where Billy is buried, I call Alf "Billy" and I think he understands that this is about remembering his brother.

I'm dreading the death of my little black cat, Sooty. She is such a star and a great talker. She's had so many accidents when the vets have thought there was no hope for her but she's survived a broken leg close to needing amputation, a punctured lung and a broken rib. She might hobble but she is one stunning cat.

When my animals die I do the manly thing and go with them to the vet. I hold them on their way in to be put to sleep and I carry their bodies home. I'm not very good at this but I do it. I can't not. Once a month we put flowers on Billy's grave and I think of him and miss him greatly.

Benson was an investment, which paid us dividends. I

bought her with Hedges and a number of others not long after
I'd bought the business in 1995. Benson weighed 22 pounds and
cost me twice as much as all the others. We lost Hedges in the
floods of 1998 but Benson survived and flourished, growing to
64 pounds. She'd hang out with another carp, as is their nature,
in an eight-acre lake. She was a handsome creature. Her scales
were perfect, and outlined black as if by an eyeliner pencil.

Her size and beauty brought to the lake anglers from all
over the world who'd come wanting to have their picture taken
with her in their arms. She was captured 63 times and I was
there for about 20 times, though I've never had my picture taken
with her. I think she got to understand the procedure – that she'd
be cradled on a rubber mat, photographed and then put back in
the lake, all within the "safe" time of ten minutes.

I got a call when I was away in Norfolk that she'd been
found floating on the water. I was devastated. It's a terrible sight
to behold a dead fish in the water. Fish are so graceful when they
swim and then when they die . . . I rushed back to help take her
from the water and bagged her up for the freezer. We hope to
discover how and why she died but, in any event, we're going to
have her mounted in a glass case and placed in the lodge where
people come to buy their tickets.

Since her death we've had loads of phone calls and the website has been overwhelmed with messages of sympathy. And when *The Times* ran the story I thought what other country in the world would have a picture on its front page of a dead carp? Only in Britain. But it's better than a lot of what's in the papers.

I'm thinking of naming the lake after her. And perhaps holding a special fishing tournament in her memory.

I remember being told by an old fisherman that if you see your fish jumping out of the water, clearing or cleaning out their gills, then you can rest easy that you've got happy fish. The time to worry is when they're skulking in the water. I like to think that Benson had a good life and was a very happy fish.

☆

Fish'n'dips

☆

B. B. Edwards

☆

There was once
a big and brave carp
Who broke many
a fisherman's heart.
Caught 63 times,
On film and by line,
Now in heaven,
she plays a mean harp.

AT HIGH TIDE the fish eat ants; at low tide the ants eat fish.

Thai proverb

Muria the donkey

Peter Chege, Manager for The Brooke, Ethiopia, Africa

I grew up in central Kenya, about 50 miles from the capital, Nairobi. I was the son of peasant farmers who grew maize and beans and kept a few cows and goats. For two years we also had a donkey, named Muria, which means the strong one. Muria carried many heavy bags between one patch of land we farmed and another about 30 miles away. I liked Muria because he made my own load lighter. He was a beast of burden and we grew up, as had generations before us, not thinking about his suffering through being beaten or overloaded. In fact, we grew up believing that donkeys felt no pain.

Remember, I'm talking third world and poverty, where cats and dogs are working animals. Cats keep away the rats; dogs are let out of their cages at night to keep away bad people. These are not places like others in the world where animals are friends, even family members. The sole reason cows and goats tend to have a better life is because they bring a double benefit: they're working animals and then they're sold for slaughter. No one eats donkeys. When they're no longer of any use they're taken to the lake and left for the hyenas.

Now I know better. I work in Ethiopia for The Brooke, an international organisation reaching more than 500,000 working equine animals each year worldwide. It works within communities providing free veterinary treatment for working equines and advising owners on short- and long-term animal care and maintenance.

I was lucky. I had a disagreement with my father when I was 13 and left home. I was begging on the streets of Nairobi when I was found and funded to go to a good school for destitute boys funded by Save the Children UK. I was well educated, given a sense of discipline, and found love. It was like going to heaven.

I worked for UNICEF for 28 years, travelling the world. I came to the UK, because I wanted to prove to myself I could work in the developed world and I did, working for several years as a manager in the NHS. My children were educated there and live there, bringing up my grandchildren. They wanted me to stay with them but I wanted to get back to where the action was.

So, I'm here now, in Addis Ababa in Ethiopia, focusing on working animals owned by the poorest people; those who, without a working horse or donkey, would go hungry tonight. There are millions of donkeys here and I've set up and trained 24 staff in three regions. Our approach is to help animal owners understand their animals' needs. You see a lot of hobbling animals, people tying the legs of an animal to restrain it, and leaving it out in the sun. I ask people to think about how they'd feel to have their legs tied together; I ask what else could be done to restrain their animals?

At market places we came up with the idea of hooks, so the animal can be tied up to the hook from a string round its neck. I ask people why they are using an umbrella to shade themselves against the sun and leaving their animal out all day in the sun? And why are they eating and drinking, and their animal isn't?

It's provocative but my own childhood experience and my regrets over Muria's life and treatment enables me to show people that treating their donkey with some thought and care could enable their donkey to live not the usual seven years but 20, and without needing expensive treatment.

The Donkey

G. K. Chesterton
1874–1936

When fishes flew and forests walk'd
And figs grew upon thorn,
Some moment when the moon was blood
Then surely I was born;

With monstrous head and sickening cry
And ears like errant wings,
The devil's walking parody
On all four-footed things.

The tatter'd outlaw of the earth,
Of ancient crooked will;
Starve, scourge, deride me: I am dumb,
I keep my secret still.

Fools! For I also had my hour;
One far fierce hour and sweet:
There was a shout about my ears,
And palms before my feet.

☆

VERY LITTLE OF the great cruelty shown by men can really
be attributed to cruel instinct. Most of it comes from
thoughtlessness or inherited habit. The roots of cruelty,
therefore, are not so much strong as widespread. But the
time must come wherein humanity protected by custom and
thoughtlessness will succumb before humanity championed
by thought. Let us work that this time may come. The quiet
conscience is an invention of the devil. Until he extends the
circle of his compassion to all living things, man will not
himself find peace. It is man's sympathy with all creatures that
first makes him truly a man.   ☆

Albert Schweitzer

1875–1965

☆

Alex the parrot
☆

Dr Irene Pepperberg, research scientist, and author of Alex & Me,
Massachusetts, USA   ☆

I was born and spent my earliest years in Brooklyn, New York.
I'm an only child and my parents and I lived above a store;
there were no other children around with whom to play. My
mother, had she been born a generation later, would have been
a career woman but in those days she did what others did and
stayed home to take care of the apartment and of me. My father
worked full time, studied hard to advance his education and took

care of his sick mother, so I never saw a lot of him.

When I was four, my father got me a budgerigar and later I'd joke that the bird was the only creature that would talk to me during the day. He accompanied me everywhere, travelling on my shoulder or a finger. He'd sit on the edge of an old-fashioned typewriter and I'd hit the heavy keys to make them ding to make as much noise as I could, and the bird would join in.

He was the first of a string of wonderful little parakeets who came into my life. Each one lasted only a few years, partly because there were few, if any, veterinarians who knew how to care for birds in those days.

I kept a budgie at college. Everyone knew about it and everyone relished Charlie Bird's personality so that his presence became an open secret. He wasn't any trouble. I cleaned up after him, he wasn't noisy but obviously when I was studying some of his feathers would get into my books and some teachers would make wry comments.

After college, I married another graduate student and we kept birds in our apartment and couldn't figure out why they kept dying. We discovered the reason when my husband was at home sick one day with the windows open and he smelt the fumes from the cars below which were being mended in the driveway during the day. Obviously, we had to stop keeping birds.

I was studying to be a chemistry professor when a series of programs came on TV about new developments in the study of animal-human communication. The programs discussed research on chimps, dolphins, whales, and birdsong, and I thought, Where's the research on parrots? *They* can actually talk. That's when I knew I wanted to give up chemistry and work in this field. Getting started was a long haul. While continuing to finish my doctorate in chemistry, I sat through seminars and classes on anything related to this new field, read copiously on these topics, and then planned a project for myself, which was when I realized it was time to purchase a parrot.

I went into a pet shop and asked the fellow working with the birds to choose one of the grey parrots from a cage of eight or nine, so I could never be accused of picking out the best, most intelligent.

Alex (for "Avian Learning Experiment") came home with me in a box. I released him into a tiny, windowless room and we sat facing one another. For several weeks neither of us felt particularly comfortable with each other.

But I began to work with Alex, discovering which objects he liked best among his toys, and using a modeling technique to demonstrate how a label could be used to obtain what he wanted. His favorite object was paper, a difficult label to produce for a creature with no lips. But he quickly started to say "ae-er". He liked keys, because he used them to scratch himself and wood because he could chew it to bits.

For 15 years he was the only bird in the research program with an army of people he came to think of as his flock. Every day for eight hours, even outside modeling sessions, at least one of us would spend the time talking to him, as one talks to a toddler, saying things such as, "Yes, you want corn. Corn is yellow." Over the course of 30 years, Alex eventually learned to identify about 100 different objects and foods; he learned labels for colours, shapes, and quantity; he learned about concepts of category, bigger-smaller, same-different, absence, and number —

he could add small quantities and even showed understanding of a zero-like concept.

Fifteen years on we brought in other parrots. At first, that was OK. We'd have a communal lunch and dinner but each bird had its own cage, its own room for training and sleeping. And Alex knew he was top bird. But then we moved to a 150-sq. ft room and Alex started dominating, interrupting the other birds, shouting out the answers when the other birds got something wrong.

I'd had Alex 30 years when early one morning I got an email to say the cleaner had found him dead in his cage. The autopsy showed he'd suffered heart arrhythmia. I was devastated. I had never let emotions muddy the lab work we did together. Of course, I cared for Alex, as one does for any colleague with whom one works for many years . . . but then, when he died, deep-seated and repressed emotions came roaring back at me.

He was cremated and I have his ashes in an urn with his name on it. I think of him an awful lot and miss him very much. He had the cognitive processing skills of a five- or six-year-old child, even if his language skills were barely that of a two-year-old, and the data we collected was ground-breaking. He'd gotten to the stage where he could manipulate me into asking the questions he wanted to answer, often to show me he was more advanced than we thought. And he could work out how to say novel words, by breaking them up into syllables. For instance, we were teaching him "seven". He began to say "s—one", leaving a space for the very difficult "v" sound. Then "s—none". Then "seben". Had he lived longer, next would probably have come "seven".

A few months after he died I began to write the book *Alex & Me*, telling our story. It was not a healing process; rather, it was

an incredibly emotional and painful experience. The book was on the bestseller list for ten weeks but I'd rather have had Alex back in my life. He was incredibly intelligent and interactive.

A year after he died a group of us had a lunch and raised a glass to him. And I remembered the closing lines from *Out of Africa*, which had been used to end *Alex & Me*.

". . . He was not ours, he was not mine. Thank you for sharing him with us. He brought us much joy. We loved him well."

I'm not sure what I believe about an afterlife. I think we're all part of nature and that individuals come into our life when they're supposed to and that interactions unfold in interesting ways. As we talk, I can imagine Alex sitting on a perch, beak tilted somewhat upward in a slightly disdainful manner, a bit put out that I've ignored him for some time, waiting for me to stroke him and pop his quills as a bird in the wild would want another to do for him to help during the molting season.

THERE IS NOTHING in which the birds
differ more from man than the way in
which they can build and yet leave a
landscape as it was before.

Robert Lynd
1879–1949

The cat opens its eyes

Anon

The cat opens its eyes
they take in the sun
the cat closes its eyes
they retain the sun
which is why come the dusk
when the cat awakes
I can glimpse in the dark
Two pieces of sun!

Tommy the tortoise, and Jeremy the tortoise

☆

☆

Diana Eccleston, writer, and a former controller for the RSPCA, south London, UK

I grew up in the 1950s with a very sweet, all-black Labrador cross, a rescue dog from Battersea Dogs and Cats Home. I was five when the vet came to the house to put him down and that was the first time I saw my father cry. I felt sad, twice over.

I was given a puppy – a dachshund, aptly named Crackers – who became fixated on my mother and would hurl himself at the door when she went out and scratch it to bits. One day, I came home from school and was told that Crackers had been given away and I was given a hamster, which I found very dull and no substitute.

Every year, we'd get a new tortoise. My mother would go to Brixton Market to buy potatoes and carrots, etc., and then, at another stall, she'd buy a tortoise for 15p in today's money. They were the focus of attention when friends came to play but the poor things were lucky to see out the year because, in those days, they were imported in sack-loads, in terrible conditions, and no one had any idea what to feed them or how to care for them.

Losing Tommy, the tortoise, was my first real and lasting experience of death. I remember sitting on the concrete by the back door, holding him and hoping the warmth of the sun would bring him back to life. My mother had to prise him away from me.

I told my brother to chip in with his pocket money to buy a companion for our new tortoise because, whatever the experts say, I was and remain convinced tortoises are happier with company. A lone tortoise is prone to wander off when it gets the urge to seek a mate. For me, the proof is the three healthy tortoises I've had for more than 40 years.

I think tortoises make a garden feel more lived in as they potter about, ploughing down the flowers, and crashing shells when it's hot and they feel randy. And I love their prehistoric appeal: old as the hills yet unthreatening in the way reptiles such as snakes and crocodiles are. They aren't exactly cuddly but they can be very friendly, charging up to you like puppies when they get to know your sound and think you have food for them.

Not that long ago, I lost Jeremy, one of my golden oldies, who died in hibernation and I'm not sure why or how. I was devastated because I loved him so much. He was small and friendly, a nice compact shape, and was always quick to put his head out of his shell for a tickle. And I was proud of him being the dad of the eggs which his partner, Titania, laid. She's a strong character, polite and ladylike. She'll wait until everyone else has had their fill before she eats. She's regal is Titania. She and Jeremy made a lovely pair.

Baby Tortoise

(an extract)

D. H. Lawrence
1885–1930

You know what it is to be born alone
  Baby tortoise!
The first day to heave your feet little by little from the shell,
Not yet awake,
And remain lapsed on earth,
Not quite alive.

A tiny, fragile, half-animate bean.

To open your tiny beak-mouth, that looks as if it would never
  open,

Like some iron door;
To lift the upper hawk-beak from the lower base
And reach your skinny little neck
And take your first bite at some dim bit of herbage,
Alone, small insect,
Tiny bright-eye,
Slow one.

The foster mum

Mary Black, volunteer, Battersea Dogs and Cats Home, London, UK

I visited Battersea Dogs and Cats Home about four years ago with a friend who was thinking of getting a dog. I hadn't realised they dealt also with cats and I wandered off to have a look. It was impressive. The cages were heated and had colourful blankets. The whole place looked cheerful and at the back of my mind, I thought that when I retired I'd like to be involved in some way. Then I saw a cat, as still as a statue, looking utterly miserable. I had to have her. I was interviewed about my home and situation, advised that this little cat might be ideal in the long run but, initially, could be big trouble. That didn't dissuade me. Neither did the fact that they had to take her out of her cage with long, industrial-strength gloves. For six months Rosie lived under a cabinet, coming out only to use a litter tray. Four years on, she's here in the room, sitting between us on a blanket, while we talk. And Rocco, my other Battersea cat, adores her.

Three near-dead stray cats have landed on my doorstep over the years, and there have always been animals in my life. One set of grandparents had a farm, my parents always had a dog, and when my children were small and because I worked, we had cats because I thought it a good idea to teach the children that if they have an animal they must care for it and respect it until it dies.

So when I gave up work four years ago, I wrote to Battersea, offering to help out in whatever way they needed. After an interview, and a tetanus jab from my GP, I became a volunteer.

I go into Battersea one day a week, as a socialiser, which means brushing and cuddling cats and kittens, and talking to them, preparing them for a life in a new home.

Battersea has four "cat" areas – reception, where new arrivals are checked out thoroughly by the vets and kept for about a week or more; mums and kittens; the isolation unit, where no volunteer who has pets at home is allowed; and the sales department.

It was about a year ago when I overheard the kennel staff talking about a particular cat and her six kittens. Fostering is an important element in Battersea's work: some long-stay animals go downhill suddenly; they get depressed living in cages. I must have mentioned that I had a spare room . . . within 24 hours, the family had moved into my house, with a large transporter cage and the food that Battersea provides to fosterers, and a list of emergency contact phone numbers.

What was it like? Well, the mother of my current litter taught her brood to use the litter tray at a very early stage, but with the first family there was pee everywhere so I learnt to cover the floor with newspaper and use a lining underneath! But they're adorable; huge time wasters as you sit and play with them, and watch them develop. They certainly have more visitors than I normally get. And Rosie and Rocco don't mind, as long as their little lives are not interrupted.

Cats behave differently when they become mothers. As

 well as a new litter, which can be demanding, they're always hungry, always on the look-out for food. And at Battersea, as well as being a stray, lost, or brought in by owners who can no longer care for them, they're coping with different surroundings, which change again when they're fostered out. It can all be quite unsettling, so they need a lot of care and understanding.

After about six weeks, the mother of my first litter was ready to return to Battersea; the weaned kittens followed a few weeks later. That was a terrible, terrible time. I cried my eyes out. I'd got very fond of them, and I missed them a lot, even though I was glad not to do the work. After nine weeks, I did and do feel possessive about them all. No matter how ordinary some might be, I think they are all stars. And, yes, I never think any owner is going to be good enough! It is a form of bereavement. I cry a great deal every time I have to have one of my own cats put to sleep. But I tell myself that I've given them as good a life as I could and being put out of pain is something we humans can as yet not ask for.

One gets over it. And I remind myself of the reason why I foster: to give a home to animals, especially ones with large litters; to give them peace and quiet, and room to thrive and play; a more natural environment that more easily acclimatises and socialises them.

Do I get tempted to keep one? Yes! But in my house, I couldn't have three cats and foster. So, I tell myself I can't have them but that I am giving them the best start in life that I possibly can.

✩ Little Paws

Anon

This is a prayer for little paws
All up and down the land:
Driven away, no friendly voice,
Never an outstretched hand.

For weary little paws of beasts
Torn and stained with red,
And never a home and never a rest
Till little beasts are dead.

O God of homeless things,
look down
And try to ease the way
Of all the little weary paws
That walk the world today.

Judge the dog

James Barnett, vet consultant to British Divers (BDMLR),
Cornwall, UK

I got my love for dogs from my mother and grandmother. There were always dogs at home, in coastal Wales, mid and south, and I helped my grandmother who bred and showed Pekingese; characterful little beasties. I studied environmental biology at Aberystwyth, switching to do veterinary science, and after a year in general practice got a job at Whipsnade and became interested in the work of the British Divers, a UK-based organisation that rescues stranded and sick marine life. I work now full-time as a pathology vet in Cornwall for DEFRA, and in my work for British Divers I help to provide advice for vets and lay people if they find a sick or injured marine creature on a beach.

Of all the animals I've known over the years at home or through work, the one that has touched my life the most was, undoubtedly, Judge, a Newfoundland/collie cross, a handsome black and white beast with a full coat and a very heavy Newfi head, who had the most easygoing, friendly and stable temperament.

For a number of years, when I worked as a company vet and travelled the country, he came with me in the car. From Scotland to Cornwall, he went everywhere and never once sat down. He stood the whole way, swaying comfortably on the corners, watching the traffic. Sometimes we slept overnight in the car. For me, on these journeys, having him with me, was immensely comforting; it wasn't like having a member of my family with me, it *was* having a family member with me. We'd stop off for great walks and everywhere we went he'd make friends instantly.

He was a rescue dog about seven or eight years old when we took him on. And we had him for 10 years. He'd belonged to the manager of the seal sanctuary where I was working. And when the manager left suddenly, Judge kept returning to the sanctuary and all round it was felt the best thing for him was to come and live with us. So he moved into our small flat, taking over the place like an oversized hearthrug.

Judge loved everyone, and everyone loved Judge. There was one time only when he ran off, chased along a cliff path, and bit someone. I believe something had unsettled him, that he felt there was a threat of some sort. He wasn't a ball-oriented dog, nor did he chase sticks and stones. He enjoyed sniffing, following scents, and if he could've climbed trees, he'd have been up there, chasing squirrels.

Judge was with us when our children were born and he died when Imogen was seven and Madeleine was 18 months old, and both have distinct memories of him. He was getting doddery with age, and the walks were getting shorter. We'd take him into the field behind the house where there were ponies. One day there was a scatty beast that just ran at and through him, bowling him over. I carried him to the house, put a drip on him and stayed with him all night. Next day I took him to the vet and, as well as internal bleeding, the X-ray showed he had cancer.

It was a time when all my professional understanding went out of the window. I sought advice from a colleague, and my wife, and I decided finally that it was better for Judge if we called it a day. I was with him when he was euthanased, and I was devastated. I took him home and that night dug a big hole in the garden and buried him, and while a party raged next door I was crying my eyes out. The next day we had a ceremony, the four of us, the children put flowers on the grave and we paid our last respects. And Madeline said, "Judgie dead, gone to heaven." Very discerning for one so young.

About 18 months later, I got a new job and we moved house and we all went to say goodbye to him. The people who bought the house sold it within a year and it's a regret to me that I didn't cremate Judge and bring him with us to our new home. I do have a faith and I do have a sense, a feeling, that Judge will be with us in some afterlife. In what way, I can't say.

We now have another dog, Alfie, a golden retriever. Oddly, Alfie has the exact same temperament as Judge and interacts with us in the same manner. The only difference is that Alfie does chase balls.

Loyalty

Anon

Y ou can't buy loyalty, they say,
I bought it though, the other day.
You can't buy friendships, tried and true,
Well, just the same, I bought that, too.

I made my bid and on the spot
Bought love and faith and a whole job lot
Of happiness, so all in all
The purchase price was pretty small.

I bought a single, trusting heart
That gave devotion from the start
If you think these things are
Not For Sale
Buy a brown-eyed puppy with a wagging tail.

Doodles the duck, Zoe, Hector, Gemma, Poppy the dogs, Orrin Prince the horse, and the white stag

Fran Lockhart, Partnerships Manager, John Muir Trust, Munlochy, Ross-shire, UK

I was born and spent my early years in Renfrewshire but the place I call home – the place dynamite alone could shift me from – is where I live now, the Black Isle, a peninsula in the Scottish Highlands, just north of Inverness. It has a beautiful coastline, unspoilt beaches, wild wooded areas, arable and stock farming, wide, slow-moving big rivers on either side, with a backdrop of mountains. It's also full of wildlife including pine marten, red squirrel, wildcats, hares, roe deer, osprey, red kite and in the surrounding firths otters and bottle-nosed dolphins, which you can see 10–15 metres from the shore playing and going mad doing back flips.

My father was an engineer, building boats and railways, and my mother was a tracer, a human photocopier before the machines were invented, and I have two older brothers and an older sister. I was named after St Francis because my parents liked animals and caring for them. There were always a couple of dogs and cats around, budgerigars, chickens, tortoises, canaries, pigeons, as well as any waif or stray that landed on our doorstep. One such creature was Doodles, a lost Mallard duckling who adopted my bare feet as his surrogate mum until he fledged and flew off to join his wild relatives.

The first dog I remember was Zoe, a brown, black-eared beagle-cross-Cairn who looked like coconut matting. I think my parents regarded her as my canine nanny. I'm not sure she was a willing volunteer but I loved her because she was small like me and was always there. I was about five when it became obvious that 14-year-old Zoe had reached the end of her days and, as my parents said, "had to be put to sleep". I imagined rows of shelves with sleeping dogs lying peacefully on them. It took me a few weeks to realise that whatever else the term meant, Zoe wasn't coming home. I was very unhappy.

Hector was my first dog. He was a rescue dog, a real mix – Labrador, greyhound and Staffordshire – and I chose him because of his rich amber eyes, unique ears, honest face and willingness to "give a paw". I had him for 16 years from when he was nearly three. He was a real character, known by the local shopkeepers and neighbouring farmers as he went on walkabouts, perhaps testing the warmth of different firesides. Hector had no killer instinct and was very protective of his squeaky toys, an orphaned baby rabbit I found, and the three kittens that our cat delivered and which worried him enormously when they mewed for their mother. When the kittens were ready to move on, Hector raced round and round the car that would take them to their new home, fretting terribly. So, obviously, we kept one to keep him happy.

Hector was hale and hearty until the last two weeks of his life. My parents were dog sitting as I was working away from home. They phoned to tell me his time had come and, to this day, I regret that I wasn't there with him at the end. It makes no difference that this happened some years ago, I keep a picture of Hector on a wall in my home but the one in my heart is clearer as it captures his soul, too. He is talked about to this day by people he "adopted" as chums. I like to think of him being with Gemma, a lurcher mix and his constant companion of 12 years. She was a quiet self-contained individual, my unassuming shadow and a solid, dependable, loyal friend.

There was dear Poppy, with her open, kindly, trusting face. She oozed gentleness. An incurable illness took her from us after a few weeks but I take comfort from the fact she was able to enjoy the May sunshine on her back, race through the wood with my pack, and splash in the river, chasing sticks. Her collar, with its name-tag, hangs in the lead cupboard and has done for 20 years. I could not bear to part with it.

I worked with horses for about 20 years and I had my own horse, Orrin Prince, for 25 glorious, adventurous years before he passed away at the grand age of 28, surrounded by his equine pals.

I was in my 30s when I decided on a career change and went to college to study conservation management. It was brilliant and when I finished I got a job surveying the footpaths in Essex. There are thousands of them and I was getting paid to inspect them as well as walk them with my two dogs, Uisge (Gaelic for water and which the English misheard as "whisky") and Astra, a lurcher we named after the car we were driving behind when, as a seven-week-old puppy, we picked her up from a rescue centre. She is so fast we should've called her Ferrari or perhaps Porsche. She was nicknamed the Electric Hedgehog because of her coarse coat and sharp little teeth and claws, but as a mature dog she seems to consider herself descended from the gracious hunting dogs depicted in tapestries in stately homes.

As well as Astra, now 11, our household today consists of Boycy, an elderly mix of poodle, Shetland and collie, who can still jump three-foot gates and chew his way through shed walls and the electrical wiring in my car; Charlie, a King Charles spaniel, who came to us "portly" and with a reluctance to go walking but is now as fit and lean as a greyhound; and Jake, who jumps out of bed every morning with a facial expression saying, *What fun shall I have today and who is going to join me?*

Oh, and as well as my partner, Mark, there's my 18-year-old daughter, Ashley, who's had a variety of pets including Pickles the rat, and Henry, a tiny hamster with a big personality. And we have eight bunnies who live outside in an area about 15 m x 15 m, with the ability to roam free if they choose.

I work with the John Muir Trust, a wild land conservation organisation, and I travel around more than 25,000 hectares and work in partnership with the owners of a further 50,000. Occasionally on my travels, I stop to take a walk with a dog or two and once, after a meeting on the west coast, I came across a rare, white stag. It was a thrilling experience. He was full grown, about six or seven years old, but not yet fully mature (nine or ten), and was just hanging out with the boys. The small herd got wind of me and moved off. I climbed a hill, so they could neither see nor smell me, and sat on a rocky knoll with my collie, Jake, quietly beside me, and took pictures of this magnificent ghost-like creature.

The Celts consider the white stag to be a potent, magical figure, like a unicorn, which heralds a major change in a person's life and a curse on the person who kills one. There's a Scottish dance named The White Stag of Aran and one traditional story tells that a white stag will appear near Brodick Castle when one of the Hamilton chiefs dies, to lead him to the other side.

I'm not religious but I love the thought that when I die all the animals I've loved will be there waiting for me, but I don't think the white stag would be there. And I wouldn't want him to be. He's a truly wild animal, a free spirit like myself, and should be off with his own kind. But it'd be nice to see him once more, from a distance, on a hill, like he was on that day.

☆

The White Stag

(an extract)

Ezra Pound
1885–1972

'Tis the white stag, Fame, we're a-hunting,
    bid the world's hounds come to horn!

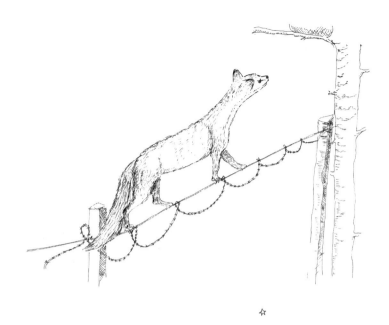

✰

Captain Corelli's Mandolin

(an extract)

✰

Louis de Bernières

✰

"There it is," she proclaimed, "it's the funny cat, and it's still tired."

"It's not tired, *koritsimou*, it's got caught on the wire. God knows how long it's been hanging there." He went down on his knees and peered at the animal. A small pair of very bright black eyes blinked back at him with an expression that bespoke an infinity of despair and exhaustion. He felt moved in a manner that struck him as quite strange and illogical.

It had a flat, triangular head, a sharp snout, a bushy tail. It was a deep chestnut colour, except for the throat and breast, which was of a shade that had settled at some indefinable point between yellow and creamy white. The ears were rounded and broad. The doctor peered into the eyes; the suspended creature was quite obviously near to death. "It's not a cat," he said to Lemoni, "it's a pine marten. It could have been hanging here for ages. I think it would be best to kill it, because it's going to die anyway."

Lemoni was overcome with indignation. Tears rose to her eyes, she stamped, she jumped up and down, and, in short, forbade the doctor to kill it. She stroked the head of the animal and stood between it and the man to whom she had entrusted its salvation. "Don't touch it, Lemoni. Remember that King Alexander died of a monkey bite."

"It's not a monkey."

"It might have rabies. It might give you tetanus. Just don't touch it."

"'I stroked it before and it didn't bite. It's tired."

"Lemoni, it's got a barb through the skin of its stomach, and it could have been there for hours. Days. It's not tired, it's dying."

"It was tightrope walking," she said. "I've seen them. They walk along the wire and they go up that tree, and they eat eggs in the nests. I've seen them."

"I didn't know we had any down here at all. I thought they stayed in the trees on the mountains. It just goes to show."

"Show what?"

"Children see more than we do." The doctor knelt down again and examined the marten. It was very young, and he imagined that it had only opened its eyes a few days before. It was exceedingly pretty. He decided, for Lemoni's sake, to rescue it and then kill it when he got home. No one would thank him for saving an animal that killed chickens and geese, stole eggs, ate garden berries, and even rifled beehives; he could tell the little girl that it had died on its own, and perhaps he could give it to her to bury. He peered round and saw that it had not only impaled itself on a barb, but that it had actually managed to wind itself around the wire twice. It must have struggled relentlessly, and it must have endured an excruciating torment.

Very carefully he grasped it behind its neck and rotated the body. Hand over hand he unwound it from the wire, conscious of Lemoni's head right next to his own as intently she watched him. "Careful," she advised.

The doctor winced at the thought of the lethal bite that might leave him foaming at the mouth or lying in bed with his jaw locked. Imagine it, risking one's own life for the sake of vermin. The things that a child could make one do. He must be mad or stupid or both.

He held the animal belly upwards and inspected the wound. It was solely in the loose skin of the groin and would have done no muscular damage. It was probably merely a question of acute dehydration. He noted that it was a female and that its smell was sweet and musky. It reminded him of a woman sometime during his maritime days, a smell to which he could not fit a face. He showed it to Lemoni and said, "It's a girl," to which she replied, inevitably, "Why?"

Dr Iannis placed the expiring animal carefully on the kitchen table and contemplated it. He took off one of his boots, grasped it by the toe, and raised it above his head. Such a small and fragile skull would be very easy to crush. There would be no suffering involved. It would be the best thing to do.

He hesitated. He couldn't give it back to Lemoni for burial with a smashed skull. Perhaps he should break the neck. He picked it up with his right hand, placing the fingers behind the neck and the thumb under the chin. It was simply a question of pressing back with the thumb.

He contemplated the deed for a few moments, exhorted himself to the act, and felt his thumb begin to move. The marten was not only very pretty, but also charming and inconceivably pathetic. It had barely lived as yet. He put it down on the table and went to fetch a bottle of alcohol. He bathed the wound carefully and put a single stitch in it. He called Pelagia.

She entered, convinced that her father had seen her kissing Mandras. She was preparing an obdurate defence, her face was flushed, and she fully expected an explosion. She was entirely amazed when her father did not even look up. He demanded, "Did we get any mice in the traps today?"

"We got two, Papakis."

"Well, go and dig them out of wherever you threw them, and grind them up."

"Grind them up?"

"Yes. Mince them. And bring me some straw."

Pelagia hurried out, both perplexed and relieved. She said to Mandras, who had been nervously kicking stones round the olive tree, "It's all right, he only wants me to mince some mice and find him some straw."

"Jesus, I said he was a funny fellow."

She laughed: "It only means he's got some new project."

Sparky the rat

Kelham Salter, sports policy researcher, London, UK

I was about nine when my mum took me to a pet shop. I wanted something a bit different, that no one else at school had, and that didn't intrude because my dad isn't that keen on animals. And there were these tiny newborn rats, the cheapest pets in the shop. My mum was a bit taken aback but they looked so sweet . . .

So Sparky came home and was with us for about four years. She lived in a cage in my bedroom and every day, when I came home from school, I let her out. She was unbelievably tame, with a defined personality. I'd say she had the character of a friendly dog. She loved attention. She'd sit on my shoulder or in the pocket of my jumper. And I know 100 per cent that she recognised me, and my mum. I cooked her whole chocolate cakes, the only thing I could cook. I might have had bits of the cake but I cooked it for her.

When I went off to boarding school, Mum looked after her. Mum loved Sparky every bit as much as I did and fed her Weetabix and milk, or bread soaked in warm milk. Sparky might not have cost very much and she was certainly very low maintenance, but when she developed cancer, twice, it was out of the question that she'd be put to sleep. My mum would not let that happen. Sparky had proper operations, the works. The vet had never known anything like it.

Sparky died one Monday after I'd returned to school, and was buried in our garden. I had another rat but I didn't feel the same about her, she just wasn't Sparky. Sparky was part of our household, part of our family.

✧

The Rat

Edwin Arlington Robinson

1869–1935

As often as he let himself be seen
We pitied him, or scorned him, or deplored
The inscrutable profusion of the Lord
Who shaped as one of us a thing so mean—
Who made him human when he might have been
A rat, and so been wholly in accord
With any other creature we abhorred
As always useless and not always clean.

Now he is hiding all alone somewhere,
And in a final hole not ready then;
For now he is among those over there
Who are not coming back to us again.
And we who do the fiction of our share
Say less of rats and rather more of men.

✩

The Wind in the Willows

(an extract)

Kenneth Grahame

1859–1932

"This has been a wonderful day!" said he, as the Rat shoved off and took to the sculls again. "Do you know, I've never been in a boat before in my life."

"What?" cried the Rat, open-mouthed. "Never been in a – you never – well, I – what have you been doing, then?"

"Is it so nice as all that?" asked the Mole, shyly, though he was quite prepared to believe it as he leant back in his seat and surveyed the cushions, the oars, the rowlocks, and all the fascinating fittings, and felt the boat sway lightly under him.

"Nice? It's the *only* thing," said the Water Rat solemnly, as he leant forward for his stroke. "Believe me, my young friend, there is *nothing* – absolutely nothing – half so much worth doing as simply messing about in boats . . ."

Louise the dog

Francis Rossi, lead singer, Status Quo, south London, UK

I was born and grew up about a dozen miles from where I live now. There was my mother, my father who was a carpenter and laid floors, and my younger brother who is now my accountant. My grandparents on both sides were retailers, in ice cream, and my paternal grandparents had dogs, mostly Pekingese. I remember Bruno, Chiefy and a black and therefore rather valuable bitch called Sweetheart. I remember Chiefy had a thing for Sweetheart, most especially one Christmas when the rest of us were sitting around, trying to play cards.

I was married at 18 and a Pekingese became a standard birthday present for me but my 21st birthday present was a faun-coloured Great Dane. She became one great big dog, although she'd always try to cuddle up to you even on the most compact of chairs. She was magnificent and I called her Louise. I loved it when people came to the house; I'd call out her name and they'd look down and along at the floor, expecting a tiny morsel of dog to be ferreting about, and in would bound this titan of a beast who seemed to appreciate the shock and disbelief her entrance had caused.

For a time I also had two wolfhounds who were lovely to look at but worked on slow burners. Oscar was a fantastic chap, who'd follow me everywhere, and there was Seamus, who was a sackful of nerves with nerves, who'd freak if anything new and therefore suspicious appeared in his world. The only time

I thought there was anything in his head was when he groomed himself along a long hedge in the garden; he'd walk down the path so the shrubbery scratched and smoothed one side, and then return the other way, repeating the exercise. I'd congratulate him and he'd preen. One day I came home and my wife said that they were fighting over her in the hall, and I rushed in to find these dogs up on the hindquarters, trying to kill one another. I realised that one of the dogs had to go somewhere else and because Seamus was too fragile to be moved, it had to be Oscar.

At my old house I had a three-acre garden, which an elderly chap, Dusty, helped me maintain. He always said that Louise was a good Christian dog. I'm not sure I knew what he meant but I've always felt she was the special dog in my life. She'd hold me, gently, by the wrist and that's how we'd walk round the garden together. In the same manner, she'd walk my mother to church and then go and collect her to bring her home. One day Louise

went missing and we couldn't find her anywhere. A few days later Dusty found her body caught on a fence; she'd been unable to reach the newly lowered neighbouring ground. She must've had a lonely, lingering and painful death, unable to bark to raise the alarm. It was absolutely terrible. I was beside myself with grief, and refused to have any more dogs in my life. I knew I just couldn't handle that sort of grief ever again.

In fact, it was ten or eleven years before I had another dog. And then we had a long gap, because I was often away on tour. Then my wife, Eileen, said that it was time to have a dog, because our three young children were the right age and if we kept on putting it off, they'd have left home. So, we've had Honeybun, a creamy golden Labrador, about six years, and two years ago we got Molly, a little white West Highland terrier – my daughter says you can see the Scot in her in her profile, and she's right. Honeybun and Molly are inseparable and adorable, and I talk to them all the time as I've talked to all my dogs, while I kid myself I'm never going to grieve over them as I grieved for Louise.

I don't like dog hairs and I don't like the smell of wet dog but you can't get away from the fact that dogs add a huge amount to your life. I don't feel my house or my life would be quite right without them.

Will the dogs be with me in an afterlife? I find it fascinating that we sit and watch the likes of *Star Trek* on TV and accept all these weird and wonderful concepts about time and space and yet there are so many people who find it hard to accept that when we die, humans and animals, we all return to a core. "As it was in the beginning . . ." So, yes, I do believe that, in some shape or form, we'll all be together as one. Me, Eileen, my eight kids, my brother, my older sister who died when she was eight hours old, my folks, along with Louise and each and every one of our dogs.

Dog, my friend

Anon

When God had made the earth and sky,
The flowers and the trees,
He then made all the animals
And all the birds and bees.
And when his work was finished,
Not one was quite the same.
He said, "I'll walk this earth of mine,
And give each one a name,"
And so he travelled land and sea,
And everywhere he went,
A little creature followed Him
Until his strength was spent.
And when all were named upon the earth,
And in the sky and sea,
The little creature said, "Dear Lord,
There's not one left for me!"
The Father smiled and softly said:
"I've left you 'til the end.
I've turned my own name back to front
And called you Dog, my friend."

Tic the dog

Simon Fremgen, schoolboy, Texas, USA

I live in a house with a garden in the middle of a big city – Austin, the state capital of Texas. My mom is a midwife and my dad is a musician and a professor at the University of Texas, and I have a brother, Jacob. We have a dog, Rufus, a Lhasa Apso, who is very excitable. My mom says he is rambunctious. We did have another dog, the same breed. She was called Tic and she died in a house fire 18 months ago. My mom and dad were at work, and Jacob and I were at school. We think there was a lit candle near the TV and the dogs were wrestling and knocked everything over. The firemen found Rufus behind the couch. He was fine. The firemen found Tic lying in the bathroom. She hadn't been burnt, she'd been suffocated by the fumes. Mom, Dad and Jacob buried her in the garden. I didn't go to her funeral. I was too upset.

Tic was born at Christmastime in the car bringing Mom and Dad's friends to visit us. She was the only puppy in the litter and she came to us when I was about three or four years old. And she was called Tic because she had a little nervous tic. She was the best Christmas present. I like small dogs and she was so cuddly. She had a very, very nice nature. She'd come over to me if she thought I was upset or she saw me crying. And she was very protective: she disciplined Rufus when he growled at me or my friends. I had a friend who grabbed her ball. Tic got it back and bounced it over and over again – like she was playing football. She was a very, very smart dog.

When we went visiting the place where Tic's mom lived, Tic'd know before we got there where we were going. She'd get very excited, whining and shaking in the car, and then she'd run about in the garden with her mom and her mom's sister, Ella.

When Tic died, I couldn't sleep some nights. I was so sad. I'd go talk to my mom, or my dad, or my brother. It helped. I know that Tic fell asleep before she died. And I know she knew we all loved her . . . I don't understand why people keep their dogs captive in rooms or why they dump them. Why can't they tell someone they don't want their dog? Why can't they find someone to adopt their dog?

It's 18 months since Tic died. I think she's in heaven now, maybe playing doggy football. I feel a lot better about what happened but I'm not over it fully. I still love her and miss her lots. We lost most everything in the fire, including our photographs, but I have pictures of Tic in my heart.

On a Clear Day

(an extract from his autobiography)

David Blunkett, MP for Sheffield Brightside, UK

Meeting Teddy was an amazing experience. The sheer size of him compared to Ruby (a previous dog) warmed my heart. Here was a dog whose body was so far off the ground that I was bound to feel if he were trying to pick scraps off the pavement or his movements indicated that he had become distracted. Here was a dog – a chocolate-coloured, curly coat retriever/Labrador cross – who needed brushing, but did not shed golden hairs all over the carpet, furniture and my trousers. Here was a dog who appeared not to be obsessed with food and took a genuine interest in where I wanted to go. My sort of dog. He was big and magnificent, and also extremely fast. Immediately we began training together I started to lose weight . . .

I was constantly astonished by Teddy's willingness to work and his dedication to getting the job done: looking out for my needs rather than his own, plodding along when the going was easy and searching out the best ways when it was difficult . . . Teddy was a workaholic, which made us well matched . . .

Teddy had been with me for the best part of nine years and was already well known in the Palace of Westminster. Having learned by trial and error to find our way through the vast maze of corridors and staircases, we had soon mastered our regular routes sufficiently to allow us to go about our business with reasonable confidence and aplomb. With my election as an MP,

Teddy was set to become the first dog allowed on the floor of the Common's Chamber proper.

There was, however, a dark cloud hanging over us: Teddy's declining health due to old age. Could he withstand the long hours and pressure of my first year in Parliament? Even at the age of eleven, his commitment and loyalty made him as eager as ever for work. Whenever the lead and harness were taken off their hook, he would be beside me, putting his head into his harness rather than waiting for me to pass it over his head. It was deeply touching. He was determined not to be left at home or to give up. He was less robust than in his youth and slightly stiffer in the joints, but otherwise not in bad shape.

After soul-searching discussions with the GDBA (Guide Dogs for the Blind Association), and since the vet assured me that Teddy was in no serious discomfort, it was agreed that he should continue working as long as he was keen to do so . . .

As the weeks turned into months, tiredness took its toll: I was struck down with viral pneumonia, which led to a spell in hospital . . . had it not been for the fact that I was forced to spend time in hospital recuperating, thereby providing an enforced rest for Teddy, I doubt whether he could have gone on working for me as long as he did, for by this time I had

noticed he was beginning to slow down. I left hospital in March 1988 under doctor's orders to take things easy, and in the weeks that followed Teddy and I made our way round Westminster looking for all the world like a pair of geriatrics.

Then one hot, humid day in the middle of May, I noticed that Teddy was panting, not abnormally at first, but as the day faded and the air temperature dropped, he seemed to grow much worse. Desperately concerned, I carried him out of the Palace of Westminster and took him in a taxi to the nearest vet.

The prognosis could scarcely have been worse. Teddy's heart and circulation were failing – he had only a few weeks to live. I literally dropped everything and with a heavy heart took Teddy by train back to Sheffield. There I left him with Valda and Trevor, who I knew would love and care for him . . . I reluctantly returned to London, where I tried my best to concentrate on the tasks in hand. It was not easy.

On 5 July, as the House of Commons was debating a motion on the fortieth anniversary of the National Health Service, I was given a message that Teddy had been rushed to the vet after collapsing and losing the use of his legs. The vet felt that he had at last come to the end of the road and that it would be kinder to put him to sleep. I had to return home at once. Without waiting for permission to be absent from the vote, I caught the next train north. When I arrived at the surgery, Teddy tried to get to his feet and I will never forget the sound of his paws scrabbling on the bare lino of the surgery floor. My heart went out to him. Despite some reluctance on the part of the vet, I managed to persuade him to allow us to take Teddy home to familiar surroundings. I did not want Teddy's days to end there in that surgery.

Once out of the car Teddy found the strength from somewhere to make his own way into the house and on to his favourite rug. When the vet arrived a couple of hours later, I cradled Teddy's head in my lap and gently fondled his ears as he was put to sleep. There is a lump in my throat as I write even after all this time. I have to admit that on that evening, with all the memories of Teddy flooding back, I became the sentimentalist I had so scorned in others twenty years earlier, before I had a dog . . .

In the days following Teddy's death, as the news spread, many kind friends and colleagues expressed their condolences, but none was more unexpected than a handwritten message from Margaret Thatcher saying how sorry she was that Teddy had died and that she understood what a great loss it would be for me, not only for practical reasons but also for the loss of the enormous affection guide dogs have for the owner . . .

Teddy had become equally widely known outside Parliament and so many sacks of letters arrived from sympathetic members of the public that a fund was set up in his memory. This raised over £7,600 for the GDBA and helped provide training for several new guide dogs, one of whom was to be named Teddy. I am sure "the gentle giant" would have liked that since he had no sons of his own.

☆

On dogs: THEY NEVER TALK about themselves but listen to you while you talk about yourself and keep up an appearance of being interested in the conversation.

Jerome K. Jerome 1859–1927

☆

George the tortoise

Peter C. H. Pritchard, Chelonian Research Institute,
Oviedo, Florida, USA

I live in central Florida in a fast-developing area near Orlando. My wife Sibille and I have a three-story, wooden 120-year-old house on an acre of land. We have a tiger-striped Abyssinian cat, Abigail, who jumped into our house and life during a heavy rainstorm, adopted us on the spot, and is very vocal in making her demands known and her welfare met.

The Chelonian Research Institute is across the road from the house and includes two houses, dating from the 1930s and 1950s, and contains the world's third largest collection of turtles – all salvaged, none sacrificed for science. In the 10 surrounding acres, mostly forest but with some old orange groves, there are gopher tortoises and box turtles, white-tailed deer, American turkeys, ten species of snake (so far), armadillos, raccoons, possums, and other fauna.

I was born in England and saw my first turtles in the London Zoo (Regent's Park) when I was five or six and decided then and there that they were unusual and worth further attention. At that time, there weren't many reference books available on the subject, apart from Gadow's 1901 book on reptiles and Gunther's 1877 book on gigantic land tortoises. When I was eight, I got my first tortoise, a Greek tortoise, which we called George for no particular reason. He had a two-tone shell, with black markings on a buff background. I bought him from a pet shop in Ealing Broadway for seven shillings and sixpence and my mother took me straight back to the shop to ask what we should give him to eat. I learnt a lot from George over the year or so I had him but finally he escaped. I like to think he's still out there, somewhere in the gardens to the west of London. This may be a forlorn hope, but sometimes tortoises do live for a very long time, the very lucky ones reaching a century or more.

I was nine when I moved with my parents, two brothers and sister to the city of Belfast in Northern Ireland where my father had been appointed Professor of Anatomy at Queen's University. We always had cats but no dogs, except for a brief experiment with a puppy we called Hagen, which persisted in bringing home our neighbour's socks, slippers, underwear, etc.

I kept turtles at Oxford, where I studied chemistry for four years before I moved to the USA (in 1965) because there was little potential to pursue my turtle interests seriously in Britain. But I'm immensely proud that the luxury, leatherbound edition of my book on the turtles of Venezuela resides in the Magdalen authors' section of the Old Library of Magdalen College, sharing a shelf with a multi-volume first edition of Gibbons' *Rise and Fall of the Roman Empire* and not far from the works of Oscar Wilde, the Duke of Windsor, Lawrence of Arabia and many other distinguished Magdalen authors.

I now have four giant tortoises, each weighing nigh on 200 pounds, any one of which can get through 20 pounds of strawberries – or hibiscus leaves – in one day. We get daily donations of yesterday's fruit and vegetables from our local supermarket, which introduces a desirable randomness into what they will get to eat on any given day – artichokes, mangos, or bananas, whatever's in season and still looking good enough for human consumption. And there's plenty of high-fiber leaf material on site, which gives them a truly varied diet.

There are three Galapagos tortoises: Moses came from the Gladys Porter Zoo in Texas, and "the twins" (not really, but from the same egg clutch) were transferred to us from the Philadelphia Zoo a few years ago. Now they are 11 years old, and too heavy for one person to lift. We also have a tortoise from Aldabra Island in the Seychelles, which we named Bernice after my wife's elder sister, because they both smile with pleasure and anticipation at the sight of food.

The four tortoises go into a retreat together but otherwise interact only minimally with each other, apart from an occasional "challenge", when they square off to see who can reach the highest. When the sun comes out, or people come visiting, they emerge in a slow stampede, sometimes crawling over each other in the hope of commandeering the feeding tray first.

If you turn on the hose and spray him, Moses will rise up as high as he can, his eyes closed in ecstasy. He'll even interrupt his feeding for this luxury. Bernice, on the other hand, is very responsive to human touch: if you simply stroke her with the lightest touch, she'll lift herself up, stretching her legs and neck as high as she can reach, encouraging you to scratch her neck.

The many varieties of turtles intrigue me but I don't have a favorite; it is their sheer variety, in size, structure, and color that is so fascinating. I like their benign demeanor, the look in their faces and their jewel-like eyes. After spending time with the giant tortoises, you learn to slow down to their pace – highly therapeutic after a hard day at the office. And they may look clumsy and burdened by a decidedly awkward body plan, but somehow it works, and has done so for millions of years.

Turtles vary in adult size from four inches to six or seven feet, and that unique, encased body plan is flexible enough for them to have learned to live everywhere that the sun is warm enough to hatch their eggs – the oceans, the deserts, swamps, ponds, rivers, prairies and forests.

But now, I worry for their future.

Having visited some 90 countries over the course of 40 years, I am unhappy seeing plastic carrier bags littering remote villages in Africa, or being eaten by leatherback turtles in the oceans of the world – the bags can be mistaken for their favorite food of jellyfish, and they have no way of coughing them back up when they discover their error. And now that humanity has burdened the atmosphere with the carbon dioxide from the combustion of millions of tons of trees, then coal, then oil during the last few centuries, I am truly uneasy that it will be too late to restore a balance to our unique Planet Earth.

Maybe a relationship with a turtle isn't the intense, emotionally bonding relationship it can be with a dog or a cat, but one can become a good friend of one's turtles, and the friendship can be a very long one. With mammalian pets, one usually has to accept the certainty of bereavement; with turtles, it is like a lottery with even odds as to which of you will go first.

Do I believe that my animals will be with me in an afterlife? My grandfather, a missionary in India in 1910, would have been cross with my uncertainty. But with so many different theories around us as to which is the true god and whether there is an afterlife – invariably proffered by those who have no basis for their certainty – I think I'll deal with that question when the time comes. In the meantime, there is much to do in the here and now.

✩

Alice in Wonderland

(an extract)

Lewis Carroll
1832–1898

"Once," said the Mock Turtle at last, with a deep sigh, "I was a real Turtle. When we were little, we went to school in the sea. The master was an old Turtle – we used to call him Tortoise—"

"Why did you call him Tortoise, if he wasn't one?" Alice asked.

"We called him Tortoise because he taught us," said the Mock Turtle angrily. "Really you are very dull! Yes, we went to school in the sea, though you mayn't believe it. We had the best of educations – in fact, we went to school every day—"

"*I've* been to day-school, too," said Alice. "You needn't be so proud as all that."

"With extras?" asked the Mock Turtle, a little anxiously.

"Yes,' said Alice: "we learned French and music."

"And washing?" said the Mock Turtle.

"Certainly not!" said Alice indignantly.

"Ah! Then yours wasn't a really good school," said the Mock Turtle in a tone of great relief. "Now, at *ours*, they had, at the end of the bill, 'French, music *and washing* – extra.' "

"You couldn't have wanted it much," said Alice: "living at the bottom of the sea."

"I couldn't afford to learn it," said the Mock Turtle with a sigh. "I only took the regular course."

"What was that?" inquired Alice.

"Reeling and Writhing, of course, to begin with," the Mock Turtle replied; "and then the different branches of Arithmetic – Ambition, Distraction, Uglification, and Derision."

"And how many hours a day did you do lessons?" said Alice.

"Ten hours the first day," said the Mock Turtle: "nine the next, and so on."

"What a curious plan!" exclaimed Alice.

"That's the reason they're called lessons," the Gryphon remarked: "because they lessen from day to day."

✩

WE CAN JUDGE the heart of a man by his treatment of animals.
Immanuel Kant 1724–1804   ✫

Tiger the dog, Thula the elephant, Saida the bear, and Malooh the tiger

Lawrence Anthony, wildlife conservationist, Zululand, South Africa

My dad worked setting up insurance offices in Zimbabwe, Malawi and Zululand so I grew up in a succession of tiny little towns surrounded by African bush. We had lots of dogs. I remember Jasper, a beautiful cocker spaniel, and my dog, an Alsatian, named Tiger. I couldn't wait to get out of school, which I found very boring, and at the end of the day Tiger and I would meet up with the black children in the village. We'd go off exploring, looking for birds and animals.

What I saw decided me on wanting to work with animals in the bush but, although that was always my hobby, for many years it wasn't possible to earn a living that way. So I worked in commerce, in property, until ten years ago I was able to buy this game reserve of 5,000 acres called Thula Thula, which means peace, serenity. You say it softly to settle a baby; if you say it loudly, it means "shut up!"

We have everything here except lions and cheetahs so we've got elephant, rhino, giraffe, buffalo, leopard, antelope, monkey, baboon, and 350 species of birds. The land was owned once by the great Zulu king, Shaka, who ruled at the time of Napoleon, and whose empire was of a similar size.

My life has been and is now devoted to animals but I'm a

practical rather than a soppy person about them. But I have a tremendous affinity and empathy with them, and an understanding and a great respect for them. That's why we work to rehabilitate troubled, traumatised elephants. We don't tame them, we work to stabilise them and re-settle them into the wild within our reserve. They are extremely intelligent and very family oriented and there's a lot we can learn from them. And, yes, the trauma they suffer comes from poor interaction with man.

About two years ago one of our elephants gave birth to a huge baby, whose front feet had been bent over in her mother's womb and she couldn't stand up. The herd of females used their bodies to shade the baby from the heat of the sun and used their trunks to support her while she suckled her mother. But after 48 hours, the herd's matriarch obviously decided enough was enough and led the herd away to the river. Only the mother and

calf remained – and you don't readily approach a nursing elephant. But, exhausted after a difficult birth, she was near to collapse.

Slowly, a few metres at a time, I managed to tempt away the thirsty, weak mother with a full can of water in the back of my Jeep. That enabled my rangers and the vet to put the baby in the back of the other Jeep and race off to put her on a drip immediately. I watched the mother return to the spot where she'd left her calf, search for an hour and then go to rejoin the herd.

It's a 24-hour job looking after a baby elephant: someone has to be there all the time, day and night, to be the surrogate parent. We rigged up sacking on a winch, the closest we could get to mimic an elephant, and hid underneath with a bottle and Thula, as we named her, began to feed. This is what you must do with an elephant, unlike a rhino who'll run you over to get at the bottle. Eventually, within a month, Thula could stand, take a few steps and walk, albeit with a pronounced limp.

She was doing really well, even following after my wife, Francoise, especially when she was cooking. And then one day Thula just stopped eating, which experts say can often happen at this stage of recovery. Whatever we did to tempt her, she wasn't interested. Her eyes grew listless; she lost weight. The vet concluded that she was in a lot of pain in her legs. And during one night, she died. Everyone gathered, we were all heartbroken, especially Francoise. Thula had gone through so much and was doing so well. But I think, with the pain, she'd decided, *Enough! I'm out of here!*

In 2003, when the war broke out in Iraq, I felt compelled to go and help the animals in Baghdad Zoo. I didn't go for the zoo, I don't like or approve of zoos, I went for the animals. I couldn't believe that animal-loving nations such as the UK and the USA hadn't got any contingency plans to help the wildlife.

When I eventually reached Baghdad Zoo, instead of 600 animals and birds, there were 50 in a very poor condition. There was no food, no water, or medicine. The hygiene was appalling, and 30–40 looters appeared at any one time.

We also raided Hussein's palaces to rescue the lions, tigers and cheetahs from dying in their cages. I had to make a difficult decision – to shoot the animals or go out in the streets and buy donkeys to slaughter them for food. It was a difficult decision but I made the choice to fight to save the wild animals. Our job was trying to build a world with broken straws.

There are two animals I recall particularly from that time. One was Saida, an Iraqi brown bear who was completely blinded by cataracts. She was an old bear, about 30, and she didn't know what was happening but with her acute hearing she heard the bombing, the shooting, the looting, and was so traumatised she paced up and down her cage the whole time. My heart went out to her.

I paid her special attention, bringing her food every day, and when the water came back on, I used the hosepipe to bathe her every day. She loved that. A British company offered to move her to a sanctuary in Greece where her cataracts could be removed but the Iraqis said she was too old to undergo surgery or be moved. So, with the US soldiers, we built her an outside shelter, a pool in which she could lie, and put in tree trunks for her to use as scratching posts – none of which she'd enjoyed before.

But she died and I still feel angry that this was no place for her, or any animal, to be – in the middle of a bloody war.

The other animal was Malooh, a magnificent Bengal tiger. He was a young adult and exceptionally good-looking. I don't know how long he and the others had been without water but when we gave them water they were so thirsty, their mouths so parched, they couldn't lap. They had to immerse their heads in the water to loosen their palates. I admired Malooh immensely; he'd been through so much, yet retained a dignity, which demanded respect. And when his strength returned, he looked beautiful, especially when the sun shone on his body. His recovery was a particular victory for us.

I returned home after six months in Baghdad and the night I left the US soldiers held a party in the zoo. One of two drunks put their hand into Malooh's cage, to pet or feed him, and got his arm mauled. The other pulled out a pistol and shot the tiger. The zoo staff had gone home and the Iraqi security staff had no means of contacting them. Malooh bled to death.

There's no word strong enough to sum up that man's action; there was nothing to justify that act of killing an animal in a cage.

This false division that has crept in between nature and man is really very damaging. We've tried to conquer nature and now we've overwhelmed it but really, our relationship is symbiotic. We survive through and because of nature. We're all in this together.

And there's hope: we get city kids, 9- to 15-year-olds, especially from the US, whose parents say they are only interested in computer games. They spend a week here, they don't want to leave and the games remain unpacked in the cases.

The Tyger

William Blake

1757–1827

Tyger! Tyger! burning bright
In the forests of the night,
What immortal hand or eye
Could frame thy fearful symmetry?

In what distant deeps or skies
Burnt the fire of thine eyes?
On what wings dare he aspire?
What the hand dare seize the fire?

And what shoulder and what art
Could twist the sinews of thy heart?
And, when thy heart began to beat,
What dread hand and what dread feet?

What the hammer? What the chain?
In what furnace was thy brain?
What the anvil? What dread grasp
Dare its deadly terrors clasp?

When the stars threw down their spears,
And water'd heaven with their tears,
Did He smile His work to see?
Did He who made the lamb make thee?

Tyger! Tyger! burning bright
In the forests of the night,
What immortal hand or eye
Dare frame thy fearful symmetry?

☆

Calypso Dancer the horse

☆

Mary Middleton, accountant, Buckinghamshire, UK

☆

As a child growing up in south London suburbs, I always wanted a dog but my mother flatly refused and it wasn't until I was in the sixth form at school that I got to know a dog which belonged to my boyfriend's family. They lived on the edge of the countryside, and I realised that was the life I wanted – country, walks and a dog.

I've had about seven dogs but, that said, for nearly 30 years of my life I had a horse, the perfect pet for a working person. A dog is wonderful but it's like a pre-school child that never grows up – you always have to be there for it. But a horse can be liveried, and someone else does the mucking out, grooming and feeding.

I took up riding seriously at university, choosing a college well out of London, and rode most evenings and weekends in Windsor Great Park. After that, I went twice a week to an extremely unorthodox riding establishment where you jumped everything, galloped, or charged through rivers. One day, the owner put me on her sister's pony, and from then on I never wanted to ride another horse and, for 30 years, rarely did.

I felt so safe and secure on her and, despite the fact that I fell off her time after time and that she was a cranky, irritable and wilful beast, she gave me confidence. Riding her was like getting into your favourite armchair.

She was 10 years old, 14.3 hands, a grey Connemara, and was called Calypso Dancer, among other things. The day they told me she was for sale, I went to the bank, and bought her that evening before they changed their minds.

She could turn on a sixpence, but only left-handed, and had two speeds: fast and stop. I remember one day, riding her in an open boggy ploughed field, when I waved through three racehorses. She chased after them like a thing possessed. I couldn't hold her back, and she kept going hell for leather over this terrible terrain until they'd disappeared from sight, at which point she pulled up, drenched in sweat.

She was getting older, losing her footing and getting panic attacks, when there was an incident when she was seriously spooked by a puddle and tipped me off so I was under her feet. I was injured, but it could've been much worse. I'd never been nervous of her in our 20-year relationship, but I was then.

I found an ideal retirement home for her and I rode her only in spring and autumn when the weather was temperate, and she was settled and happy. Then one winter she developed a sore on her backside which grew bigger and wouldn't heal, and the vet said, with spring approaching, and flies, it was better to let her go. The light had gone out of her eyes, she couldn't lift her head or her tail, and I couldn't bear it. I'd always been there for the dogs but . . .

The traditional method is to shoot horses; an injection can cause them to panic when their legs give way. Either way, I decided I couldn't cope. I went to work and left it to the vet, and to Calypso's stable girl. They told me she sank gently to the ground. I try not to think about it, but I hope that's how it really happened. I always gave her the best – cost and conventional wisdom didn't come into it.

Not long ago, I was out for a walk when I realised I knew exactly what it would feel like to be riding her across this unknown field with a curving track. It doesn't matter to me that I'll never ride again, I'll never lose that feeling; I'll never lose her. She is always there, in my consciousness.

✧

A CANTER IS the cure for all evil.

Benjamin Disraeli 1804–1881

Prayer of a Horse

Maurice Portal

"To you, my master, I offer my prayer. Feed me, water and care for me, and when the day's work is done provide me with shelter, and a clean dry bed, and a stall wide enough to lie down in comfort.

"Talk to me, and your voice often means as much to me as the reins.

"Pat me sometimes, that I may serve you more gladly and learn to love you. Do not whip me when going up hill, never strike or kick me, but give me a chance to understand your orders.

"Watch me, and if I fail to do your bidding, see if something is wrong with my harness or feet.

"Do not tie my head in an unnatural position or take away my best defence against the flies and mosquitoes by cutting off my tail, or limit my range of vision by blinding so that I am frightened by what I cannot see. And finally, O my master, when my youthful strength is gone, do not turn me out to starve or freeze, or sell me to some cruel master to be slowly tortured or starved to death.

"But do you my master take my life in the kindest way and your God will reward you here and hereafter; you will not consider me irreverent if I ask you in the name of Him who was born in a stable."

Satira the horse, Cleopatra, Flora, Flora 2, Lili and Daisy the dogs, and NettieByrd the parrot

Bonnie Wyper, entrepreneur, New York, USA

I was born and raised in West Hartford, Connecticut with my sister and two brothers, and pets were very much part of our lives. I was always bringing home waifs and strays, little field mice or birds, which often didn't make it and always devastated me. Every summer we went to stay with my grandparents on their 400-acre farm in Buffalo, New York, some eight hours' drive away where my grandfather bred horses and also prize-winning chickens, which my great-grandfather showed in Madison Square Garden. I love chickens to this day. They remind me of a simpler existence when people lived on farms and killed only what they ate.

I got my first dog when I was 12. Cleopatra became the first of my three beloved English bulldogs. To me they are incredibly appealing dogs; funny, packed with personality, sweet-tempered, and loyal, they remind me of my mother's sister, my Aunt Ada, who had Down's syndrome. It took me years to understand why I identified with them until I realized that they're big personalities in a medium-sized package – a bit like me! Cleo would chase around and if you reprimanded her, she'd go and sit in the corner, her head facing the wall. I think she had a sense of ironic humor! She was five or six when she began suffering from seizures. My mother took her to the vet and Cleo never came back. It was devastating and I weep now at the memory. It was what people did back then. They didn't spend fortunes on medication the way they do now. The vet thought it was incurable encephalitis. I realize now it was epilepsy, which is common to the breed.

I took riding lessons and every summer on the farm I rode Satira, a beautiful white horse who inspired me to want to become a jockey. I loved her and wanted her with me all year round so I persuaded my family to board her near to our home. The day after she arrived, we went away on a fortnight's holiday and returned to find that Satira had been put down by the stable while we were away. They said there was something wrong with her hooves. I look back now and think it was probably laminitis, an inflammation of the hooves, and there was no choice other than euthanasia but, at the time, I was absolutely devastated. Satira was my pal and container of my dreams, closer to me than my siblings.

Years later, my partner and I raised another English bulldog, Flora. She was like our kid. She came everywhere with us and everyone knew her. She became the mascot of the gallery I was running at the time. She had all the lovely qualities of her breed. When I left the gallery, I became a radio broadcaster for a period of time. Many of my shifts started at 4.30 a.m, which meant rising at 2.30 a.m. Flora hated being walked in the dark and let that be known by peeing in the same place in the living room every day. When I left the job, she stopped the peeing. She was 13 years old, living with my mother, when she had a heart attack.

Not long after my mother died, I got another English bulldog. I was living in New York at the time, and called the new dog, Flora 2. She was very pretty and voted the most popular dog on my block by the various doormen, but she was not more than three or four years old when she began to suffer from epileptic seizures – some of them lasting up to 20 minutes. She would lose control of her bladder and bowels. It was absolutely devastating for me and for her, and I eventually had to put her down because the seizures became uncontrollable. It was the hardest thing I've ever had to do. I still cry thinking about it. She was cremated and her ashes put into a bowl and the vet made a donation to a charity in her name. I took her ashes and buried them in Central Park and drank a toast to my gentle pal.

Now I live with NettieByrd, a 13-year-old Caique parrot, who I've had since she was a chick, and two pit-mix dogs, Lili and Daisy. I take the dogs to Central Park each morning to have a good romp (they are allowed off the leash until 9 a.m.) and have met all kinds of other dog owners, some of whom have become good friends. It's the canine equivalent of the morning school bus stop as a social incubator. I dread losing Lili, who I've had for 10 years, perhaps because her kind, caring and watchful nature reminds me of my mother. It's why I got Daisy five months ago. I'll be able to share the sadness with her.

Do I believe in an afterlife where I'll meet up with my pets? I don't know. I believe in some form of reincarnation, that our molecular structure is reassembled in some way – which might explain why certain people resonate with you when you meet them and others not. You may well have known them in another lifetime as a different person. Perhaps it's the same with pets. I do think my pets chose me rather than the other way around. But for the moment, while I'm on this earth, I'm putting my energies into creating a lecture series highlighting new scientific discoveries about animal cognition and behavior so as to make people aware of the connections and similarities between humans and animals. It seems to me that we need to get more people involved on a personal level in animal welfare and conservation if we are going to prevent the unconsciousness and atrocities that are leading to the exploitation and extinction of so many species. It's a way of saying thank you to all the animals I've been lucky enough to know.

☆

Black Beauty

(an extract)

Anna Sewell
1820–1878

Joe Green went on very well; he learned quickly, and was so attentive and careful that John began to trust him in many things; but, as I have said, he was very small for his age, and it was seldom that he was allowed to exercise either Ginger or me. But it so happened one morning that John was out with Justice in the luggage-cart, and the master wanted a note to be taken immediately to a gentleman's house about three miles distant, and sent his orders for Joe to saddle me and take it, adding the caution that he was to ride carefully.

The note was delivered, and we were quietly returning till we came to the brickfield. Here we saw a cart heavily laden with bricks. The wheels had stuck fast in the stiff mud of some deep ruts; and the carter was shouting and flogging the two horses unmercifully. Joe pulled up. It was a sad sight. There were the two horses straining and struggling with all their might to drag the cart out, but they could not move it; the sweat streamed from their legs and flanks, their sides heaved, and every muscle was strained, whilst the man, fiercely pulling at the head of the fore horse, swore and lashed most brutally.

"Hold hard," said Joe, "don't go on flogging the horses like that; the wheels are so stuck that they cannot move the cart." The man took no heed, but went on lashing.

"Stop! pray stop," said Joe; "I'll help you to lighten the cart, they can't move it now."

"Mind your own business, you impudent young rascal, and I'll mind mine." The man was in a towering passion and the worse for drink; and so he laid on the whip again. Joe turned my head, and the next moment we were going at a round gallop towards the house of the master brickmaker. I cannot say if John would have approved of our pace, but Joe and I were both of one mind, and so angry that we could not go slower.

The house stood close by the roadside. Joe knocked at the door and shouted, "Hulloa! Is Mr Clay at home?" The door was opened, and Mr Clay himself came out.

"Hulloa, young man! you seem in a hurry; any orders from the Squire this morning?"

"No, Mr Clay; but there's a fellow in your brickyard flogging two horses to death. I told him to stop and he wouldn't. I said I'd help him to lighten the cart, and he wouldn't; so I have come to tell you. Pray, sir, go." Joe's voice shook with excitement.

"Thank ye, my lad," said the man, running in for his hat. Then, pausing for a moment – "Will you give evidence of what you saw if I should bring the fellow up before a magistrate?" he asked.

"That I will," said Joe, "and glad too." The man was gone, and we were on our way home at a smart trot.

"Why, what's the matter with you, Joe? You look angry all over," said John, as the boy flung himself from the saddle.

"I am angry all over, I can tell you," said the boy, and then in hurried, excited words he told all that had happened. Joe was usually such a quiet, gentle little fellow that it was wonderful to see him so roused.

"Right, Joe! you did right, my boy, whether the fellow gets a summons of not. Many folks would have ridden by and said 'twas not their business to interfere. Now, I say, that with cruelty and oppression it is everybody's business to interfere when they see it; you did right, my boy."

Joe was quite calm by this time, and proud that John approved of him. He cleaned out my feet, and rubbed me down with a firmer hand than usual.

They were just going home to dinner when the footman came down to the stable to say that Joe was wanted directly in master's private room; there was a man brought up for ill-using horses, and Joe's evidence was wanted. The boy flushed up to his forehead, and his eyes sparkled. "They shall have it," said he.

"Put yourself a bit straight," said John. Joe gave a pull at his necktie and a twitch at his jacket and was off in a moment. Our master being one of the county magistrates, cases were often brought to him to settle, or say what should be done.

In the stable we heard no more for some time, as it was the men's dinner-hour. But when Joe came next into the stable I saw he was in high spirits; he gave me a good-natured slap and said, "We won't see such things done, will we, old fellow?" We heard afterwards that he had given his evidence so clearly, and the horses were in such an exhausted state, bearing marks of such brutal usage, that the carter was committed to take his trial, and might possibly be sentenced to two or three months in prison.

It was wonderful what a change had come over Joe. John laughed, and said he had grown an inch taller in that week; and I believe he had. He was just as kind and gentle as before, but there was more purpose and determination in all that he did – as if he had jumped at once from a boy into a man.

✧

THE WIND OF heaven is that which blows between a horse's ears.

Arabian proverb ✧

✧

Creature and The Enforcer the ✧ cats, and Griffin the dog

✧

Sheri Soltes, Founder & President, Texas Hearing and Service Dogs, Austin, Texas, USA

I was born in Boston, Massachusetts and raised in Madrid, Spain and Dallas, Texas, moving around as my father, who was in the air force, studied medicine. I'm the eldest of three: my brother is now a doctor in Houston and my sister is an attorney here in Austin, but before they arrived on the scene, we had a cat called Creature.

As we moved about, I had to make new friends and Creature was a constant in my life and felt like a sibling. The fact that she never wanted to be petted, let alone touched, and was a great hisser never bothered me. I didn't know that cats could be any different. Nevertheless, she made me aware at a very early age that I'd always make time to pet a cat, even if I was in an evening dress and had to crawl under a car.

I was seven and Creature was 20 when my mother accidentally backed the car over her and killed her. I lay down on the drive next to Creature and cried over her body. I'm sure that through knowing her I developed a soft spot for alley cats or rough-and-tumble animals, which don't fit the norm.

One came into my life much later, when I was living in Houston and had just set up THSD. He was a beat-up, much-wounded former feral, known in the neighborhood for charging dogs. For months I left out food for him and eventually he let me touch him. The first time he played with a toy was an utter joy. I called him The Enforcer Cat. He was a brave and confident cat who turned into a loyal, affectionate friend. When he died, I did what I always do when I've lost an animal: I wrapped his body in an old, much-loved sweater. We buried him under a wheelchair ramp, which we'd built to help clients into my office in the house. Somehow, it seemed appropriate.

I studied law and wherever I was living, I'd bring in strays or feral cats. In fact, I had a boyfriend test: if we were out driving, I'd tell them to pull over if I saw a stray cat so we could pick it up. If they didn't stop . . . well, it led to relationship meltdown.

I practised law for eight years in Houston in the 1980s. I worked for a highly esteemed law firm, which I grew to admire because it fought tooth and nail for the underdog – injured workers or their families. But for me, being a lawyer was boredom punctuated by stress. I wanted a job where I felt fulfilled. Then I read an article about rescue dogs helping people with disabilities. I founded the THSD and for two years worked at it part time, while continuing as a lawyer. Now, it's been a full-time job for 20 years and I definitely feel fulfilled. I've found my calling: turning strays into stars.

We've helped about 500 people and all our dogs come from animal shelters or rescue groups. If they turn out not to be suited to this work, we find the dogs a home where they'll be a pet. We never return them to a shelter. It takes eight months to train a dog and three/four months to train a person to work with the dog. We have a dedicated training building where people attend classes for a week, working with the dog and a trainer, and then the trainer spends 13 weeks visiting the person and the dog at home, working with them as a team in their home, office or school, and their community, ironing out any difficulties, such as the refrigerator which opens the opposite way from the one we have in-house, which might require some retraining.

Our teaching program is one of positive training, rewarding good behavior. We use no force or aversive techniques. Part of my policy is giving each a dog a positive name, such as Noble, Glory or Diamond. I have a monthly spot on a TV program called *Café Woof* about how this really works and teaching positive training to the public. One topic debunked the use of choke chains, shock collars and the rest, which are evil as well as useless. And this reminds me of one of our dogs.

He was an Austrian Shepherd/Border collie cross we named Blue because one eye was half brown, half blue. He'd been with his new partner, a teacher, about two weeks, at the beginning of their 13-week in-home training period. Chris, a delightful, handsome young man who's in a wheelchair with spinal injuries following a car accident, took Blue for a walk in the park. Going down a hill, the electric wheelchair toppled over, with him strapped to it. There was no one in sight and Chris had to let Blue off the leash to find help, which after 20 minutes he did, returning with a woman he'd somehow convinced must follow him. Blue had got his freedom; he could've run away, but he didn't. Even in the early stages of their relationship, there was a bond, which I believe was there and in greater abundance through positive reinforcement training. I like to quote the American psychologist, Abraham Maslow: "There's no such thing as a well-adjusted slave."

All the dogs we have are lovable and I wish we could adopt more. And although I'm a cat person, I love having a dog, and it helps to take one out and about to demonstrate the work we do. And, yes, one became my soul mate. I called her Griffin, because she looked like a mythical beast. She was a Briard mix, except her ears didn't stick up, with a mass of shaggy grey hair. She was a cheerful, happy dog, nice to cats, and a wonderful companion. I'd jog round the city's big lake with her at my side, and people would turn, and call out, "What is *that?*" At the end of the run, she'd wade into the lake to cool down, her mass of hair surrounding her like a big halo.

She was diagnosed with lung cancer when she was 13 years old and very soon afterwards I realized she had to be euthanased. I called out the vet, lay down on the floor beside Griffin and held her in my arms as the vet administered the drug.

It's been three years now and I still keep a notebook on my nightstand. Each night before I turn out the light, I mark another day that she's been gone, putting a star against the days I've dreamt of her. I talk to her in my head and in my heart almost every night and sometimes when I'm jogging with my current dog. I'm sure I've got permanent curvature of the spine from accommodating her on the bed. She wasn't quite the size of a small horse but not far off it, and her absence has left a big physical as well as an emotional gap in my life.

I was brought up in the Jewish faith, which tells you how to live and behave while on earth but pretty much leaves you on your own to decide what happens to you after death. So I like to think that we get together again with our animals. Certainly, I wouldn't want to be any place without them.

☆

CHILDREN ARE FOR people who can't have dogs.

Anon   ☆

Memories

(an extract)

John Galsworthy
1867–1933

My companion tells me that, since he left us, he has once
come back.

It was Old Year's Night, and she was sad, when he came to
her in visible shape of his black body, passing round the dining
table from the window end, to his proper place beneath the
table, at her feet.

She saw him quite clearly; she heard the padding tap-tap of
his paws and very toe-nails; she felt his warmth brushing hard
against the front of her skirt. She thought then he would settle
down upon her feet, but something disturbed him, and he stood
pausing, pressed against her, then moved out toward where I
generally sit, but was not sitting that night.

She saw him stand there, as if considering; then at some
sound or laugh, she became self-conscious, and slowly, very
slowly, he was no longer there.

Had he some message, some
counsel to give, something he would
say, that last night of the last year of all
those he had watched over us?

Will he come back again?

No stone stands where he lies. It is
on our hearts that his life is engraved.

Teddy Bear the cat

Tom Boyle, retired businessman and animal rights fundraiser,
New South Wales, Australia

I was born and spent my early years in County Kerry in Ireland. My brother, eight years older than me, did have a racing greyhound but ours wasn't an animal-oriented house and I suspect the reason was economics. My family moved to England in 1946, after my mother died, and in 1951 my father took us to Australia – perhaps the best single thing he ever did for us.

My wife, Patricia, grew up surrounded by pets including Herb, a kangaroo, and when we married in 1965 my wedding present to her was a small black poodle we called Pixie. Three years later we got Boo, a beautiful white Persian cat. This was my first experience of cats and Boo taught me that cats are not like dogs, they do their own thing, in their own way, and they're not ones for taking orders.

We live now in the southern highlands of New South Wales, 120 kms south of Sydney, in one of the most verdant areas of Australia, with four cats and a horse, on five acres surrounded by large farms. We've had a number of animals but never one like Teddy Bear.

He was a spotted cream British short hair, with a big, wide face and Cheshire cat grin, and was very affectionate. Mostly, he chose Patricia's lap but he was, I felt, my cat as opposed to our cat. He had a cat's independent spirit but, more than all the others, Teddy Bear showed me the importance of living in the moment.

Not recklessly, but with an awareness to look at the beautiful things in life which we may see every day but fail to see afresh. Every day, every moment for Teddy Bear was an adventure. He'd explore familiar territory in the garden, seeming always to discover something new – different birds, frogs or butterflies, a new light or shade or perspective. I saw in him, more than any other cat, an ability to live in a constant state of meditation, focussed on the moment.

Teddy Bear was not only an adventurer and philosopher, he was a gourmet, not to say a gourmand. He loved the refrigerator, or whatever was in it. If he was in hearing distance and heard the fridge door open, he'd arrive like a rocket. As feeding time approached, he'd sit on his back legs, back against a cupboard, belly exposed, and look at you – until he was sure you'd got the message. We called him The Dishwasher because he'd clean up the plates of all the other cats.

Teddy Bear was friendly with all our animals and he loved to wrestle with Pompuss, his brother. Fur would fly but when they'd finished, they'd walk off on their next adventure.

Four years after we got him, we realised Teddy Bear wasn't well. The vet diagnosed the problem as a rare blood disease in which the immune system attacks itself. He had four blood transfusions before I read of a homeopathic treatment, which we started him on, and last year the tests showed his count was normal. The vet said it was a miracle. But this year he began to deteriorate: the disease had caused his kidneys to collapse. In the final week he slept with me and was restless and miaowing in the night, and touching my face with his paw, and so the moment came. The most devastating in my 69 years.

That morning, Teddy Bear visited all his old haunts, all the other cats, and the horse that came to the fence and nuzzled his old friend. And the vet put him to sleep. I could not stop crying. I picked up Teddy Bear and carried him round the garden. I couldn't let him go.

We buried him in the garden between two of Patricia's favourite roses. The spot is marked by a rock and on it a plaque that reads: "Teddy Bear, 22.09.02 – 04.04.07, One Brief Shining Moment".

I was brought up a Roman Catholic but now I think religion is the greatest marketing story ever sold. I do believe there's a spiritual connection of some sort and that Teddy Bear is in another dimension in some shape or form. He's a Time Lord, and some day, we'll meet again. Maybe it's my way of dealing with the loss but, equally, I believe a spirit such as his could never die.

☆

THERE ARE TWO means of refuge from the miseries of life:
music and cats.
☆
Albert Schweitzer 1875–1965

A cat's prayer

Anon

Now I lay me down to sleep,
I pray this cushy life to keep.
I pray for toys that look like mice
And sofa cushions, soft and nice.
I pray for gourmet kitty snacks
And someone nice to scratch my back,
For window-sills all warm and bright,
For shadows to explore at night.
I pray I'll always stay real cool
And keep the secret feline rule
To NEVER tell a human that
The world is really ruled by cats.

Wishful thinking

Susie Cornfield

You sit there, your striped back to me,
Nose at your peak, staring, staring,
Up, up and away.

A round red paper spot on a sold picture
And I have captured you – if only for a moment,
If only in an etching.

You remain, in body and spirit, free.
Free to enjoy delights, to face dangers
and maybe, to succumb.

I watch you, staring, staring,
Up a tree, to the fidgety squirrels,
Into the sky, at the autumn flights
Above us, off into the unknown.
What don't you know that I have no need to know?

Once, you fitted into the palm of my hand
Once, you clung to my neck with your claws,
As I cling to you now in fear.

What is it that I love and am scared to lose?
Your delicate elegance? Chocolate paws, triangular face, tigrous
    eyes?
The waving tail that flags from side to side in greeting?
Your squeaky call when you come in?
"I am here, where are you?"
Or your independence that takes you off to unknown places?

You were lost nearly to maladies unknown,
and a car which damaged your bright brain
but not your spirit.

When you climbed curtains and
Turned the household upside down,
I thought you a beast, clawing your way into my life.

Now I see you as a gift, on loan.
To be treasured and kept, 'til you are returned,
Please God, way, way overdue.

Then, brave little tiger,
I shall have you in a moment
    and only in an etching
And I shall be staring, staring
And following, following your
    gaze.
Wondering what it is you
    never knew that I have no
    need to know.

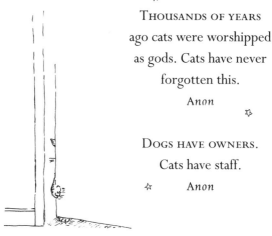

THOUSANDS OF YEARS
ago cats were worshipped
as gods. Cats have never
forgotten this.

Anon

DOGS HAVE OWNERS.
Cats have staff.

Anon

Laddy, Domino, Sammy, Fancy and Oliver, the dogs

Colleen O'Brien, Director of Communications,
PETA (People for the Ethical Treatment of Animals), Virginia, USA

I was born in Fayetteville, North Carolina and raised in Oregon on the west coast, which I consider to be home, the place where I'm rooted, the place of beautiful mountains and high cliffs overlooking a magnificent ocean. My dad was in the army but left and got a job when he realized he was going to be posted abroad and separated from my mother and me, and my younger brother and sister. When I was 18 we moved to Maryland, on the east coast.

We always had dogs and the first one I remember was Laddy, a tan and white collie, who I loved very much. I'd lie on the floor, watching TV, and he'd lie beside me; he'd sleep next to me on the bed. He was mild-mannered and laid back and he was my companion for nine years before he got sick, developed kidney problems and lost his appetite completely. I remember my mother on the phone to the vet, saying he'd have to be put to sleep. I broke down, crying uncontrollably; I was inconsolable.

While it was much less common in those days to be with your animal when it was put to sleep, to this day I regret deeply that not one of us was there with Laddy when he was euthanased.

We got a collie pup, Dusty, who died very young, of what we never discovered. My mother was heartbroken and we were dogless until a Dalmatian mix bounded into our lives. Domino was a bundle of energy; he never slowed down even when he was old. He was a real lap dog, stretching his whole body across the three of us sitting on the couch.

And then, before I went to college, I got a tan and white collie, Sammy, from a shelter. She was eight years old, in poor condition because she'd been kept outside and used for breeding purposes. Yet somehow this quiet, gentle dog, without any fight or to-do, came to rule the roost over the fiercely protective Domino. Something made him a bit afraid of her.

She came with me to college for my last two years, sharing a house with a friend and happily sitting on her back when she was lying on the floor, watching TV. She was 16 when she developed arthritis in her hips and couldn't stand easily. Her quality of life was declining and I didn't want her to suffer . . . My family came

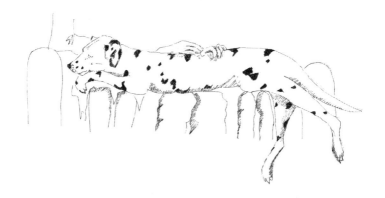

over from Maryland and one Saturday we took Sammy to the vet. I've never felt so wretched. And yet I believe the decision I took was unselfish: it wasn't the easiest emotional decision for us but for Sammy, it was the best, most unselfish decision.

Not that long after Domino fell ill. Domino had been my brother's baby and when he had to be put to sleep my mother, my brother, my sister and I were in the room with him. My brother, who was 21, broke down and wept. I've never seen him so upset, and I never want to see him that upset again.

Sammy died four years ago. I keep her ashes in my bedroom, with cards I received from friends and family, and the vet. I have two adorable cats, but at that time I didn't know if I was ready to commit to another dog. Could I love one as much as Sammy? And then, in 2005, along came Hurricane Katrina, devastating New Orleans.

With other charities, PETA went in to rescue animals and brought back to Virginia dozens of sick and homeless pets that were taken to the vet, and then found foster or permanent homes. I offered to foster a seven-year-old toy poodle whose guardian had taken her mother to the hospital, expecting to be able to return home before the storm hit.

The dog had been stuck in the house for two weeks, in chemically polluted waters. She weighed five pounds, was practically hairless, and had a uterine infection that required emergency surgery. I fell in love with her there and then. Strangely, despite all she'd been through, the fancy pink varnish on her toenails remained intact – so I called her Fancy. Her hair grew back, she gained weight, she became this amazing, playful, absolute joy of a dog, who proved immensely popular with my colleagues at work.

And then, through a dedicated rescue website, Cyrillia, Fancy's guardian, tracked down her dog, whom she called Licorice, and asked for her back. I was almost sick with grief. Cyrillia and I exchanged photos; we talked on the phone. And one day, I took a plane from Virginia to New Orleans, and after a long flight of many tears, I met Cyrillia and her family. I felt unsettled because Fancy didn't appear to be settled – until Cyrillia said to her, "How's my beautiful black girl?" Immediately, Fancy jumped at her leg: she'd recognized Cyrillia. It was a great weight off my mind. And Fancy, or rather Licorice, didn't look back at me as she headed off home.

Someone made a video of the reunion at the airport and when Cyrillia felt Fancy was a bit depressed, she'd sit her down in front of the screen, and Fancy, now called Fancy Licorice, responded enthusiastically when she saw me.

Cyrillia and I keep in touch at holidays and through photos and emails. And mine is the emergency number if there's a problem. I feel I've made a friend for ever. I was in New Orleans, on a press tour for PETA, advising people not to abandon their animals in times of extreme weather, and visited Fancy Licorice and Cyrillia who presented me with a huge bouquet of cookies, each one with the face of a different dog, with the largest cookie of all in the middle of the bunch with the face of Fancy Licquorice, and on it the words "Thank you, PETA."

I felt very lonely after Fancy returned to New Orleans but equally, loving her made me realize that I'd got a lot of love to give and a time came when I felt capable of giving it. It was Christmas and I went to an animal shelter and found Oliver, a 14-year-old, four-pound miniature Yorkshire terrier, brought in the day before by an elderly lady who could no longer care for him. The shelter rang her to say he'd been rehoused. Little Oliver can certainly hold his own against the cats and I like to think that PETA saved Fancy and Fancy saved Oliver.

As a teenager I worked in a zoo for three years and saw some animals go insane in their confined isolation. Once I held a silky Chinese chicken in my arms and talked to visitors about how great and interesting a chicken was. Suddenly, I woke up to the fact that I'd be eating one that very night. What was I doing? I wrote an essay for a competition, which won me a ticket to a PETA symposium on animal rights. I heard Ingrid Newkirk, PETA's co-founder, speak and I knew then where I wanted to be, where I wanted to work. And I haven't changed my mind.

We live in a tabloid society where many people have a short attention span and are looking only for exciting news. At PETA, we're trying desperately to change people's minds, and at times, to get a serious message across about animal welfare, we do outrageous stunts to reach the media and the people beyond.

Why? Because by treating animals in an inferior way to humans we ultimately harm ourselves. As Gandhi said: "The greatness of a nation and its moral progress can be judged by the way its animals are treated."

✦

WE NEED A boundless ethic which will include the animals also. The ethics of respect for life makes us keep on the lookout together for opportunities of bringing some sort of help to animals, to make up for the great miseries men inflict on them.

Albert Schweitzer 1875–1965

✦

Gurami the fish

James Stacey-Clear, estate agent, Surrey, UK

I'm about to lose one of a pair of guramis I bought when I set up my first tropical fish tank in my room at Northampton University four years ago. Her partner was a big orange-coloured bully who became better behaved when I introduced more fish. She used to change colour and markings from dark blue to white, dependent on her mood, but now she is old, and her fins and scales are showing signs of ageing.

My father is a keen fisherman and we always had a pond, and whenever we went to a fair, I came home with a goldfish.

But I wasn't interested in catching fish, rather with life under the water, and how you can create a fish's environment in your own room. I've learnt a lot but if a fish is poorly I ask the aquarium shop for a diagnosis and water analysis.

Keeping tropical fish turned out to be a good chat-up line. And I found girlfriends really enjoyed coming along with me to garden centres to choose a new fish. But that wasn't why I kept them. They're easy to look after and, unlike dogs, which I love, they're not going to get up to much mischief, like rooting around in bins or whatever. And they're very relaxing. I liked to watch the gurami and the others while I was studying and doing my dissertation.

Now I'm at work, the gurami lives with my 13 other fish in a large tank in my mother's hallway. Like the others, I feed her by hand. She's become less nervous, less shy, and rather clever in the way she avoids the other fish, checks out everything, and is at the front of the queue for food. I'll be sad when she dies but there's a special spot in Mum's garden where I'll bury her.

☆

ANYONE WHO HAS accustomed himself to regard the life of any living creature as worthless is in danger of arriving also at the idea of worthless human lives.

Albert Schweitzer 1875–1965   ☆

Heaven

Rupert Brooke

1887–1915

Fish (fly-replete, in depth of June
   Dawdling away their wat'ry noon)
Ponder deep wisdom, dark or clear,
Each secret fishy hope or fear.
Fish say, they have their Stream and Pond;
But is there anything Beyond?
This life cannot be All, they swear,
For how unpleasant, if it were!
One may not doubt that, somehow, good
Shall come of Water and of Mud;
And, sure, the reverent eye must see
A Purpose in Liquidity.
We darkly know, by Faith we cry,
The future is not Wholly Dry.
Mud unto Mud! – Death eddies near –
Not here the appointed End, not here!
But somewhere, beyond Space and Time,
Is wetter water, slimier slime!
And there (they trust) there swimmeth One
Who swam ere rivers were begun,
Immense, of fishy form and mind,
Squamous, omnipotent, and kind;
And under that Almighty Fin

The littlest fish may enter in.
Oh! never fly conceals a hook.
Fish say, in the Eternal Brook,
But more than mundane weeds are there,
And mud, celestially fair;
Fat caterpillars drift around,
And Paradisal grubs are found;
Unfading moths, immortal flies,
And the worm that never dies.
And in that Heaven of all their wish,
There shall be no more land, say fish.

☆

The farmer's wife

☆

Trees Fewster, Yorkshire, UK

☆

I always wanted a cat when I was growing up, the youngest of six, in an animal-free household in Amsterdam. I did have one – for about half an hour. I brought it home from a neighbour's and it weed in the corner of a room. My mother sent it back.

I came to London when I was 20 to work as an *au pair* and at the end of the contract came to Yorkshire to work for Dr Barnado's. I'd been so lonely in London that I decided I'd accept every invitation I got so when a friend asked if I'd like to visit his friend who had a farm . . .

It was only seven miles from Leeds, Bradford, Halifax

and Huddersfield, in a built-up conurbation in industrial West Yorkshire, yet from the farmhouse we could see only acres and acres of green, undulating land. When I walked into the milking parlour, there was the farmer and that was that. It was love at first sight and we married six months later.

Malcolm was 30 and the 100-acre farm then had a cat, two dogs, geese, cows, pigs, and a few sheep and hens. Very soon we added four children. I knew nothing about farms so I followed Malcolm on the farm walks he did for young schoolchildren. After a few months, I realised he was talking over their heads, assuming they knew things which I knew they didn't, and I took over.

I had to learn everything but it was very interesting. I loved it. And my life. Especially when I thought of my sister back in Amsterdam, living in a flat on the fourth floor, with no lift, a baby and another on the way, and the toilet on the second floor.

Every year, we sell about 20 of our 100 cattle. Every calf is taken from its mother 24 hours after its birth. The mother returns to the herd and the calf goes in a pen with the other calves. Because we're a dairy farm, we can't use male calves, which are either sold at market or, privately, to a beef farmer to be reared for meat. We keep the female calves to replace the dairy cows. I know the cow misses its calf as it spends usually one night crying. That's the way it is, but cows have friends within a herd and that distracts them within a day or two.

My eldest daughter did have a pet cow. She'd talk to it when she was upset and read to it. There came a time when the cow had to be put down and my daughter decided to stand by it as the deed was done. The knackerman was a bit angry but my daughter had felt close to the animal . . . I thought what she did was right.

When the children were young they put a little dead bird into a shoebox and buried it under a "tree of heaven", sang hymns and took a photograph. Death is part of life, and I'm glad they all learnt that at an early age.

A few months back, on Palm Sunday, a working dog, which belonged to my eldest son, was run over by a tractor. He had a broken leg and his working life was over. The vet couldn't be reached so, while Malcolm and I went to church, my son, who lives next door, came over with his gun. By the time we got home, my son had shot and buried the dog. I was very proud of him. And it reminded me of a time when my children were young. They're all musical and they used to perform in old people's homes. My son used to sing "Old Shep", a song about a faithful old dog which has had its day, is shot by its owner, a young boy, and goes to heaven.

Malcolm has had a series of terriers over the years. Outside, they're working dogs; inside, they're his lap dogs. He's very fond of them and feeds them titbits at the table. They don't come to me because they know I don't do that. Perhaps I'm a bit harder than my husband. I can pluck a hen and cook it, but he can't.

That said, we had a calf born blind. In a pen, Sandy learnt how to avoid things but when she grew bigger, we knew she'd never survive so she was slaughtered and put in the freezer. We all knew that we were eating Sandy. That's the way it is. The other night, I prepared a whole fish, with its head and tail, and before I put it in the oven, I showed it to my two-year-old granddaughter. She knew what it was, and I think that's the way it should be: that the fish had lived, and was killed in order for us to eat.

It's like the December, many years ago, when my eldest son was late for school, and the teacher wanted to know why. He said he'd had to catch Christmas Day lunch. That's the reality.

☆

A Farmer's Boy

Anon

They strolled down the lane together,
  The sky was studded with stars –
They reached the gate in silence
And he lifted down the bars –
She neither smiled nor thanked him
Because she knew not how;
For he was just a farmer's boy
And she was a Jersey Cow.

Chewing the Cud

(an extract from his autobiography)

Dick King-Smith

As well as cow-keeping, we began pig-keeping. The poor old pig, linked always with gluttony, obesity and squalor. As greedy as . . . as fat as . . . as dirty as . . . In fact, pigs are very like us. Their digestive systems are almost identical to ours, they are omnivorous as we are, and they very much enjoy their food, as we do. They are also intelligent, strong-willed, and of an independent nature, all gifts we admire in ourselves. We can hardly blame them for fatness and greed, since we have bred and fed them for just such qualities, licking our lips with an anticipation that is almost cannibal as we lean upon the wall of a sty and look down upon these creatures that so nearly resemble us.

As for being dirty (by which we mean not just muddy but incontinent), given half a chance there is no cleaner animal on the farm. Humans, once out of nappies, pride themselves on confining their excretions to a particular spot, as opposed to the random discharge of cattle or sheep or poultry; and they instruct the dogs and cats that share their houses to respect that privilege. But without any training the pig from an early age will use a dung passage and never soil his sty.

As for intelligence, when next you get a chance, look closely into a pig's eye. The expression in the eye of a dog is trusting, of a cat supercilious, of a cow ruminative, of a sheep vacuous. But the look in the eye of a pig is, quite simply, knowing. Other beasts think, "This human is looking at me." The pig thinks, "I am looking at this human." There is all the difference in the world.

It is a most pleasant and comfortable thing, to hang over the wall of a sty and look upon pigs. Any kind of pig is of interest, but people who work with stock learn to tell quality; and the two young boars whose backs were scratched that October morning were a picture.

Litter brothers, they stood shoulder to shoulder and grunted their appreciation of our fingers in the coarse hair of their long strong backs. Their fringed ears stood stiff, their tails curled tight, and the white lashes lay thick on their closed eyes as they swayed like belly-dancers to our touch. The price was right, the bystanding breeder reliable. All I had to do was choose.

There was nothing in it. Lord knows they had length and to spare. But perhaps one was a shade longer than his brother, and I leaned over and gently pulled his ear.

Maybe the one we left behind also had a happy and memorable life, but I'm glad I didn't take him. I'm sure he could never have been the pig that Monty was.

Something-or-other Field Marshal was his registered name, so he had to be called after that self-important little soldier. But everything about my Monty was big – his heart, his appetite, and eventually his size. Once he became too large to get into my pig-weighing machine, there was no way to gauge his weight but by eye, but before his last illness, five years later, I reckon he would have topped 600 pounds.

By that time he had had for a long while a harem of ten

Saddleback sows, roaming the dells and hillocks of The Wood. And always, when one happened suddenly upon him around a bush, or saw him come crashing through the undergrowth at the cry of "PIG-pig-pig-pig!" and the rattle of the bucket, there would be an instant of shock at the sheer bulk of him. The sows were hardly sylph-like, but when Monty covered one, it seemed that her back must break.

Yet he was the gentlest of animals. Like all his kind, he loved to be scratched, but he had two particular penchants in the matter. He liked it done on the top of his head, between his great ears; and he liked it done while he was sitting down. Perhaps in the belief that it made things easier for the scratcher, though in fact the reverse was true, he would lower his hams, place his forefeet neatly together, and sit bolt upright, eyes already closing in anticipation.

If the children were playing in The Wood and came upon him, Monty would immediately sit to attention. And though the girls could reach the tickling spot without too much difficulty, Giles at the age of four or five had to reach right up, his nose level with the boar's tusks, his face almost touching the huge snout.

I hadn't liked the look of him on the Wednesday and was worried enough to seek professional advice, but was not at all expecting what I found on the Thursday morning.

Behind the back doors of the barn was a square area, fenced of course with coffin boards, which led by way of a narrow passage directly to The Wood, and thus allowed us to move pigs between one place and the other. In the centre of this square was a hollow, the bed of an old pond. Like some African water-hole it was often bone dry, and the sows would lie on its slopes and enjoy the sun like fat ladies at the seaside. Sometimes, in the wet, it had a lovely muddy mess in it and became a wallow.

That morning there was only one animal lying stretched out on the bank of the pond. For a second I thought that Monty was simply sleeping. But somehow he seemed flattened, almost two-dimensional like a great cardboard figure, and even longer than in life. Later, when the vet cut him open, the endless length of his gut was chock full of earth, like a giant sausage. Some depravity of appetite had led him to eat the mud of the wallow until at last he was bunged up solid. Not much of a death.

I have one splendid memento of Monty, a photograph of him in his prime, taken by a press photographer who had come to interview me for an article in a local paper. Majestically, the boar sits on his great backside, and, respectfully, I squat before him on my haunches, my fingers making their customary obeisance upon his bristly brow. Some pig.

✩

ALWAYS REMEMBER,
a cat looks down on
man, a dog looks up
to man, but a pig will
look man right in the
eye and see his equal.
Winston Churchill
1874–1965

✩

The wallabies,
and Cadbury the dog

Robin Loder, Leonardslee, Horsham, Sussex, UK

I was brought up at Leonardslee, an estate of 225 acres of lakes and gardens and nine miles of garden paths and woodland walks. It has been in my family since 1889. My great-grandfather, Sir Edmund Loder, filled it with every kind of non-carnivore imaginable: deer, gazelle, antelope, prairie dog, mountain goat, emu, ostrich, kookaburra. In fact, in Victorian times, articles in *Country Life* reveal that it was better known for its fauna rather than its flora.

I just about remember beavers in the lakes when I was a child and, of course, the Tasmanian Bennetts wallabies, which have been at Leonardslee since my great-grandfather brought them here. Numbers have varied over the years, but now there are about 40. Difficult to say exactly because they won't line up to be counted. I don't see them as pets but as magnificent mowing machines and a hugely valuable part of our work force. No petrol, no wages, no overtime nor holidays, and with a replacement baby mowing machine in the pouch!

They are no trouble. They eat brambles and avoid the bluebells. They fertilise the ground with droppings as small as those of a rabbit. They have soft underfeet, which do little mechanical damage to the microflora of the ground on which they tread. They don't need or want shelters, dens, holes in the ground, or nests in trees; they live out. And they look endearing.

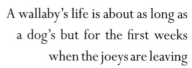

A wallaby's life is about as long as a dog's but for the first weeks when the joeys are leaving the pouch they are no match for marauding foxes.

I grew up with Labradors and when I was about 25, living in the country and able to have my own dogs, I decided to have brown Labradors, so mine would be more easily distinguishable. I take care to train them not to chase wallabies or deer. The training takes time and happens in stages, so that the dog reaches a point, hopefully, when it doesn't so much as blink if it encounters a wallaby on the hop.

My first chocolate dog, Cadbury, was trained to a whistle. I took him out to do the deer test. I sat him on a path in the Leonardslee Deer Park some 50 yards from some Sika deer and walked towards them on my own. They scattered to let me pass, and stood watching a few yards away either side of the path. When I'd gone some 50 yards beyond the deer, I called the dog to come to heel. All was going smoothly with the dog walking towards me, correctly ignoring the deer. Suddenly, the Sika deer gave their alarm signal, which sounds like a high-pitched whistle, not unlike the whistle I use. Instantly, the obedient dog sat down. At the second alarm call the dog lay down. At the third whistle, the poor dog didn't know what to do or whether the two- or four-legged creature was its master.

We went on to use hand signals but when Cadbury went totally blind we went back to voice commands. I know I'm lucky because we've got the space, but I never put my dogs on a lead; equally, they have to learn that with freedom goes a sense of responsibility.

Perhaps because I've grown up and always lived in the country, I take flora and fauna to be part of a bigger picture – the landscape. And it's the landscape as a whole that I love.

Do I believe that our animals will be with us in an afterlife? If there is anything, I cannot imagine that there will be people in people form, or animals in animal form, doing what we do on earth. But we'll have to wait and see, won't we?

☆

Verse for a Certain Dog

☆

Dorothy Parker

1893–1967   ✩

Such glorious faith as fills your limpid eyes,
Dear little friend of mine, I never knew.
All-innocent are you, and yet all-wise.
(For Heaven's sake, stop worrying that shoe!)

You look about, and all you see is fair;
This mighty globe was made for you alone.
Of all the thunderous ages, you're the heir.
(Get off the pillow with that dirty bone!)

A skeptic world you face with steady gaze;
High in young pride you hold your noble head,
Gayly you meet the rush of roaring days.
(Must you eat puppy biscuit on the bed?)
Lancelike your courage, gleaming swift and strong,
Yours the white rapture of a winged soul,
Yours is a spirit like a Mayday song.
(God help you, if you break the goldfish bowl!)

"Whatever is, is good" – your gracious creed.
You wear your joy of living like a crown.
Love lights your simplest act, your every deed.
(Drop it, I tell you – put that kitten down!)
You are God's kindliest gift of all – a friend.
Your shining loyalty unflecked by doubt,
You ask but leave to follow to the end.
(Couldn't you wait until I took you out?)

✩

You CAN SAY any fool thing to a dog, and the dog will give you
this look that says, "My God, you're right! I never would've
thought of that!"

Dave Barry

✩178✩

Teabag the dog, Ernie the chimpanzee, Lumio and Nestles the cats, and Tonka and Hickory the horses

Toby Sedgwick, actor, director and Olivier award-winning choreographer for the National Theatre production of War Horse, *Surrey, UK*

We started work on *War Horse* some two years before the first rehearsal. I'd ridden as a young boy, and you don't forget the skills, but I hadn't ridden for a long time. A neighbour kept horses in the field at the bottom of our garden and I spent many, many hours studying, filming and riding two very different animals, which had formed an unlikely bond with one another: Hickory was a perky, attention-loving individual with thoroughbred leanings; Tonka had a gentle, more rounded character.

I studied their feet, their heads, their movements and their interaction with one another and with humans. And over the weeks and months we spent in workshops and rehearsals, the puppeteers of the horse characters came to know both Tonka and Hickory extremely well.

It was the opening night when the neighbour rang me: Tonka had died of a heart attack. She must have called out in her distress because they found Hickory standing outside her stable, having broken down the door to his neighbouring stable in his attempt to reach her.

It was heartbreaking, and a shock for all of us who'd come to know these beautiful horses. Certainly many tears were shed when our neighbours eventually felt able to come and see the production, and see how much both their horses had given me in my research.

I'm lucky; there've been animals around for most of my life, except in the early years when I was getting established. For me, animals are a joy to be with and, as I'm often away working, a huge part of the thrill of homecoming.

I grew up in south London with my parents, two brothers and always a cat and a dog. My first animal memories are of Nicholas, a one-eyed Siamese cat, and Lucy, a Bassett hound, a great actress, who'd turn on the eyes to suggest the end of the world was nigh unless you fed her something.

But the closest relationship I had with an animal in childhood was when I was about 10. Ernie was a chimpanzee who worked in films, who I met with his minder in Richmond Park where we regularly walked our dogs. We spent the summer playing, Ernie and I – he performing an acrobatic feat and me copying him. It was an amazing experience, and I felt we really understood one another. Ernie would see me from across the park, shout and come running over, and not only for the bananas I brought occasionally. And I did miss him greatly when he went off to work on another film.

The first pets I owned were with my girlfriend some 30 years ago. They were two very affectionate Burmese – Lumio, a great big beautiful, amazingly graceful ginger ball who, without a fight, ruled the local neighbourhood, and who protected Nestles, a small brown cat.

We'd had them about six years when one day Lumio disappeared. We called and called but this time he didn't respond. We found him the next morning, on top of our high garden wall, his back legs broken and his claws out. He'd been run over but had struggled to get home. We couldn't bear the thought of taking him to the vet so we buried him in the garden. It was terrible, and terrible for Nestles who couldn't understand where her protector had gone. And then she too went missing. We never found a body and that's the worst, not knowing what's happened and having nothing tangible to grieve over.

I had to go away on tour soon afterwards, which makes sharing a loss and grief difficult. A few years' back it happened again, with my wife, Clare, and me.

Teabag was our beautiful black flat-coat retriever, a softie, clever and sensitive, who loved people and hated arguments. We'd had him nine years when, six months after he'd recovered fully from a severe stomach problem, he went off his food, preferring to stay indoors, curled up in a ball. And we noticed one front leg was getting weaker – beyond what we'd thought normal for a sprain. I was away, working on a TV series in Edinburgh, and was sitting outside on a sunny warm day, when I knew something was wrong. I called Clare. At that moment she was at the vets', stroking Teabag's body. Under an anaesthetic, they'd discovered that the bone in the leg had all but disintegrated with cancer and Clare was advised that it'd be kinder to let Teabag die while he was still unconscious.

I was distraught at Teabag's death, and frustrated to be away from home at such a time. The kindly producer told me to take the afternoon off, and that weekend I flew home. We buried Teabag in the garden, and Clare and I, and our two sons (Dominic, nine, and Pascal, five, at the time), each said a few words. There's a white cross with his name on and the date he died. I don't believe in an afterlife where one meets up with one's animals, but I do think a lot about Teabag and he's close by, buried at the bottom of the garden, close to the field where we used to walk when Tonka and Hickory were there.

☆

Dogs are our link to paradise. They don't know evil or jealousy or discontent. To sit with a dog on a hillside on a glorious afternoon is to be back in Eden, where doing nothing was not boring – it was peace.

Milan Kundera   ☆

War Horse

(an extract)

Michael Morpurgo

So Friedrich rode with us that autumn day when we went to war again. The gun troop was resting at midday under the welcome shade of a large chestnut wood that covered both banks of a silver glinting river that was full of splashing, laughing men. As we moved in amongst the trees and the guns were unhitched, I saw that the entire wood was crowded with resting soldiers, their helmets, packs and rifles lying beside them. They sat back against the trees smoking, or lay out flat on their backs and slept.

As we had come to expect, a crowd of them soon came over to fondle the two golden Haflingers, but one young soldier approached Topthorn and stood looking up at him, his face full of open admiration. "Now there's a horse," he said, calling his friend over. "Come and look at this one, Karl. Have you ever seen a finer looking animal? He has the head of an Arab. You can see the speed of an English thoroughbred in his legs and the strength of a Hanoverian in his back and in his legs. He has the best of everything," and he reached up and gently rubbed his fist against Topthorn's nose.

"Don't you ever think about anything else except horses, Rudi?" said his companion, keeping his distance. "Three years I've known you and not a day goes by without you going on about the wretched creatures. I know you were brought up with them on your farm, but I still can't understand what it is that you see in them. They are just four legs, a head and a tail, all controlled by a very little brain that can't think beyond food and drink."

"How can you say that?" said Rudi. "Just look at him, Karl. Can you not see that he's something special? This one isn't just any old horse. There's a nobility in his eye, a regal serenity about him. Does he not personify all that men try to be and never can be? I tell you, my friend, there's divinity in a horse, and specially in a horse like this. God got it right the day he created them. And to find a horse like this in the middle of this filthy abomination of a war, is for me like finding a butterfly on a dung heap. We don't belong in the same universe as a creature like this."

To me the soldiers had appeared to become younger as the war went on, and certainly Rudi was no exception to this. Under his short cropped hair that was still damp from wearing his helmet, he looked barely the same age as my Albert as I remembered him. And like so many of them now he looked, without his helmet, like a child dressed up as a soldier.

When Friedrich led us down to the river to drink, Rudi and his friend came with us. Topthorn lowered his head into the water beside me and shook it vigorously as he usually did, showering me all over my face and neck, and bringing me sweet relief from the heat. He drank long and deep and afterwards we stood together for a few moments on the river bank watching the soldiers frolicking in the water. The hill back up into the woods was steep and rutty, so it was no surprise that Topthorn stumbled once or twice – he had never been as surefooted as I was – but he regained his balance each time and plodded on beside me up the hill. However I did notice that he was moving rather wearily and sluggishly, that each step as we went up was becoming more and more of an effort for him. His breathing was suddenly short and rasping. Then, as we neared the shade of the trees Topthorn stumbled to his knees and did not get up again. I stopped for a moment to give him time to get up, but he did not. He lay where he was, breathing heavily and lifted his head once to look at me. It was an appeal for help – I could see it in his eyes. Then he slumped forward on his face, rolled over and was quite still. His tongue hung from his mouth and his eyes looked up at me without seeing me. I bent down to nuzzle him, pushing at his neck in a frantic effort to make him move, to make him wake up; but I knew instinctively that he was already dead, that I had lost my best and dearest friend. Friedrich was down on his knees beside him, his ear pressed to Topthorn's chest. He shook his head as he sat back and looked up at the group of men that had by now gathered around us. "He's dead," Friedrich said quietly, and then more angrily, "For God's sake, he's dead." His face was heavy with sadness. "Why?" he said, "Why does this war have to destroy anything and everything that's fine and beautiful?" He covered his eyes with his hands and Rudi lifted him gently to his feet.

"Nothing you can do, old man," he said. "He's well out of it. Come on." But old Friedrich would not be led away. I turned once more to Topthorn, still licking and nuzzling him where he lay, although I knew and indeed understood by now the finality of death, but in my grief I felt only that I wanted to stay with him to comfort him.

The veterinary officer attached to the troop came running down the hill followed by all the officers and men in the troop who had just heard what had happened. After a brief inspection he too pronounced Topthorn to be dead. "I thought so. I told you so," he said almost to himself. "They can't do it. I see it all the time. Too much work on short rations and living out all winter. I see it all the time. A horse like this can only stand so much. Heart failure, poor fellow. It makes me angry every time it happens. We should not treat horses like this – we treat our machines better."

"He was a friend," said Friedrich simply, kneeling down again over Topthorn and removing his head-collar. The soldiers stood all around us in complete silence looking down at the prostrate form of Topthorn, in a moment of spontaneous respect and sadness. Perhaps it was because they had known him for a long time and he had in some way become part of their lives.

☆

A HORSE GALLOPS with his lungs,
perseveres with his heart,
and wins with his character.

Federico Tesio 1869–1954 ☆

Cosmo the cat

Mary Harboe, radio presenter and writer, Spain

I'm a farmer's daughter and animals have always played a big part in my life and while my parents were commercially sensible and dealt with life and death on a daily basis, they were also very sentimental about their animals. Whenever there was a premature lamb it was put in the lowest part of the Aga, where one didn't cook but warmed plates, to help it survive. I'm sure this is why, as an adult, I became a vegetarian because I couldn't eat a leg of lamb without thinking this was once one of four trotting round a field.

We lived on a farm near King's Lynn in Norfolk and kept a dairy herd, and then sheep and Border collies, and I had a lovely little pony called Cobweb, but I always wanted a cat. I spent hours trying to befriend a feral cat to no avail and then, when I was about 16, a friend's cat had kittens. Neither my parents nor our dog had the merest whiff of my secret kitten, Hamlet – until the time came to take him to the vet to be "done". I'd saved up just enough money. The trouble was it turned out Hamlet, although a ginger, was a girl, and the female operation cost more than the male op. The vet very kindly did the deed for the same price. Hamlet was a wonderful friend for nine years but, although my parents cared for him very well, he never did forgive me for abandoning him during the week to go to work in London.

Over the years, and whichever country I've lived in, there have always been cats and dogs in my life and in 1993, when

I'd been living in Spain for four years, I decided I wanted a companion for Sparky, a little black and white cat we'd brought from Holland, who was getting on in years. My hairdresser had a beautiful Siamese cat, with an exotic admirer, a Persian cat who'd come from Brazil. Cosmo was one of the litter and was absolutely delightful. It was, for us both, love at first sight.

He was a soft minky grey with tiny white markings and grew into a big cat, especially when measured against Spanish cats, which tend to be small and skinny. He had the charisma of Tony Blair, the brains of Boris Johnson and the *savoir faire* of Peter Ustinov. He was a great character and even people who professed not to like cats liked Cosmo. And I know for a fact that in Barcelona there are cats named after him.

He loved running water and would sit on the lavatory seat whenever I took a bath or shower. His favourite sleeping position was on my chest, as close to my chin as possible, from where he'd gaze lovingly into my eyes. More often than not, he'd get so carried away with his feelings that he'd forget to swallow, but I never minded the dribble of Cosmo.

Although most fastidious in his behaviour, Cosmo's "table" manners left a lot to be desired. He was an exceptionally messy eater. He always ate dried food but somehow managed to leave crumbs all over the floor, near and far from his plate. And sometimes in the night I'd hear him slurping from the glass of water beside my bed. That's when I learnt to cover the glass.

He was capricious, like many cats: open the door for him, and he'd stroll off casually, deciding perhaps it was better not to go out. Close it, and he'd miaou the house down until someone came running to let him out.

For some 18 months in his later years, he enjoyed a hippy phase in student digs with my son, Thomas. You'd find him chilled and flopped out on the sofa alongside the boys, listening to loud music and live drum sets.

Cosmo was my shadow: he complained to the neighbours when I went out, and when I pulled up in my car, he'd complain to me from the balcony three floors up.

He hated cars with a passion and I vowed that when his time came, I'd call the vet to him and I wouldn't go down the road of extensive drugs or invasive surgery. I'd noticed that he was losing weight and that while he was eating and talking as normal, he was also getting slower. It was one Sunday. We'd been out in the morning and when we came back, I saw he wasn't at all well. I phoned the vet who came prepared for anything but when he examined Cosmo he found lots of internal growths throughout his body. We sat on the sofa and Cosmo was put to sleep in our arms. We buried him in the garden and put a blue-flowering plumbago on his grave.

I was absolutely devastated. I'm holding back tears as I talk to you now. He died 16 months ago, but I talk about him or think about him almost every day. Cosmo was my cat, my shadow, my best friend.

Pangur Ban

Written by an unknown monk living in the eighth/ninth century
(translator, Robin Flower)

I and Pangur Ban, my cat,
'Tis a like task we are at;
Hunting mice is his delight,
Hunting words I sit all night.

Better far than praise of men
'Tis to sit with book and pen;
Pangur bears me no ill will;
He, too, plies his simple skill.

'Tis a merry thing to see
At our task how glad are we,
When at home we sit and find
Entertainment to our mind.

Oftentimes a mouse will stray
Into the hero Pangur's way;
Oftentimes my keen thought set
Takes a meaning in its net.

'Gainst the wall he sets his eye
Full and fierce and sharp and sly;
'Gainst the wall of knowledge I
All my little wisdom try.

When a mouse darts from its den.
O how glad is Pangur then!
O what gladness do I prove
When I solve the doubts I love!

So in peace our tasks we ply,
Pangur Ban, my cat and I;
In our arts we find our bliss,
I have mine, and he has his.

Practice every day has made
Pangur perfect in his trade;
I get wisdom day and night,
Turning Darkness into light.

The vet

Peter Knapp, vet, Carshalton, Surrey, UK

I've been a vet for more than 30 years, and established Parkside Veterinary Centre more than 20 years ago. My unwritten ethos is: listen to what the owner says, however silly it sounds, because they know their pet best.

At home, aside from my wife and children, I have two dogs, two fish and a hamster. At Parkside we have five vets and ten nurses, providing on-site care seven days a week, with emergency and in-patient facilities which are air-conditioned, and under-cage heating in the stainless-steel kennel block. As well as the more usual domestic animals, the practice sees a lot of local wildlife, via London Wildcare and the public, and in my time, I've treated koi carp, wallabies, racoons, even a panther cub. I operate a global discussion list and website for vets, and discuss cases with colleagues in-house or on the list.

On average, we deal with two to four deaths a day. Some are natural, some trauma or illness, some animals are dead on arrival, some we euthanase, mostly for health reasons, but we do have cases of the biting dog or the incontinent animal where the owner can't or won't cope.

Strong bonds can develop between people and pets and these can end in painful losses, and, yes, there are special ones which get to you – mostly because animals don't judge in the same way as people. Telling people their pet is dying and should be euthanased goes with the job. If it can't be helped, I don't have a problem. It's way, way harder if there is an untoward death or a death from a procedure carrying a low but known risk.

Death is not so desperate if it's due to old age or a progressive disease or nasty illness where we're doing the pet a favour, but it's harder when it's through stupidity — a road accident, a gate left open, or garden toxins. I was more upset when my favourite young cat got run over than when another went into age-related congested heart failure and died while I was trying to help it. Equally, I was upset when I had to euthanase my first dog with a leukaemia that did not respond to radiation/chemotherapy, but it had had lots of happy years and that reconciled me.

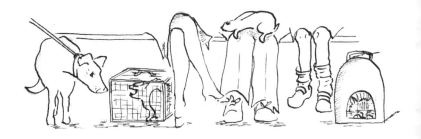

I come from the age of "It's happened, you deal with it", but my nurses are very good at talking to people. We offer options of burials, cremation, and ashes returned in assorted urns or caskets. For myself, I have no wish to keep bits of ash or fur as a memento. Call it a deficiency but, for me, it's the living pet that was the personality not the cadaver.

It's very, very rare for people to refuse permission to euthanase a sick pet and although, legally, we have the right and obligation to euthanase if we see fit, I didn't sign up to drag a pet from an hysterical owner. So, an option would be to load it with massive pain relief so that it's unaware while the owner comes to terms with reality or the animal dies. If an owner were away or uncontactable, we'd seek colleagues' opinions before we took any action. In the last resort, we'd contact a welfare organisation, such as the RSPCA, which has more legal expertise and muscle.

The people who make us groan are those who come in, patently wanting an animal euthanased and, although we can help it, that is not what they want to hear. Whatever the reason behind their intent (money, nuisance, a genuine belief that it's for the best), it seems some folk want us to carry the blame for the decision so that they can feel less guilty. They don't want to hear alternatives, referrals to charities, or treatment options. And this problem is more common than one would wish.

It takes diplomacy, but over the years we have managed to take the animal from the owner, treat it, and rehome it. The most dramatic case was a five-month-old German shepherd pup, which had a broken leg. At least the owner was brutally honest that he wasn't going to look after it and was pleased to go home without paying any bill. The dog was rehoused the same day to a very nice man and happily went home with him in her plaster cast.

✧

THE QUESTION IS not, "Can they reason?"
nor, "Can they talk?"
but rather, "Can they suffer?"
Jeremy Bentham 1748–1832 ✧

Four-Feet

Rudyard Kipling
1865–1936

I have done mostly what most men do,
 And pushed it out of my mind;
But I can't forget, if I wanted to,
Four-Feet trotting behind.

Day after day, the whole day through –
Wherever my road inclined –
Four-Feet said, "I am coming with you!"
And trotted along behind.

Now I must go by some other round, –
Which I shall never find –
Somewhere that does not carry the sound
Of Four-Feet trotting behind.

MY GOAL IN life is to be
as good a person as my dog
already thinks I am.

Anon

Henrietta the hen

Annie Rapoport, composer, Surrey, UK

I'm number three in a family of six children and we've always had pets. My earliest memories are of our cats, Pusky and Whoosky, who I recall were always in the kitchen but that may be because that's where their food was. Tocas, our tortoise, arrived when I was two. Later, we had a mouse and various hamsters including two Russians, Frank and Nordberg (named after the *Naked Gun* characters), who were not very friendly. Russian hamsters are notoriously territorial and don't like being lifted out of their cages.

I got Henrietta for my ninth birthday, with two other hens. Mummy built them a henhouse, with a run, but they were often let loose in the garden. I was very fond of them all but I was instantly mad about Henrietta. I'm not sure why. She did look different from the other two. She had lighter, softer feathers and looked cuddlier, like a teddy bear. She was approachable and sweet, confident and brave, and didn't seem to mind being cuddled. A lot of the hens we've had are difficult to approach and pick up because they're naturally suspicious – even of the people who feed them – and run away from you. Henrietta was friendly with most people. Did she recognise me? I'm not sure.

She was probably between 14 and 18 weeks old, as hens usually are when they're bought from a farm or market. Because they were "my" hens, for my birthday, I looked after them, although, looking back, Mummy probably did all the hard stuff.

But I did feed Henrietta nice bread and potato peelings. Like most hens, she loved potato peelings. And I had a book, given to me by family friends, that taught me about caring for hens.

I remember Odile, my eldest sister, laughing when she found me in the potting shed, talking to Henrietta. But I liked spending time with her, just reading or chatting, when she and the other two hens were loose in the garden.

Once we were all late for school because, as we were about to leave home, we saw the three hens up on the roof of the air-raid shelter next to our house. My sister, Izzy, who was seven, tried to explain this to her teacher but he told her off for lying and sent her to stand in the corner.

One day, when I was 11, I remember going out to the chicken run and finding Henrietta completely still and stiff and, for a few minutes, I couldn't accept that she was dead. I felt terribly sad because she was my pet and, for a hen, she'd lived a long life and I'd got used to her being around. I sat in the run for some time, and then went to tell Mummy that Henrietta was dead, all the time hoping that I was wrong and that really she was still alive.

Henrietta was one of the few of our hens who didn't meet her end in the jaws of the fox, so I know I was lucky she was around as long as she was. Mummy helped me bury her in a corner of our garden, near the pond, where we buried some other pets. I think I marked the spot with some stones.

I don't remember but I'm told that night my parents had a dinner party and I spent the whole evening sitting on the floor sobbing my heart out, with Izzy and a friend of Mummy's sitting beside me, trying to console me. I don't remember many details about my time with Henrietta but I haven't forgotten the feelings

– of loving her and of being very upset when she died.

Now that I'm older, I suppose I realise that hens are functional pets, there to provide food. They don't have long lives and it is sad when that life is cut short by a fox, but hens are not like cats, which are with you for years and years and are definitely part of the family.

Hen's Nest

John Clare
1793–1864

Among the orchard weeds, from every search,
Snugly and sure, the old hen's nest is made,
Who cackles every morning from her perch
To tell the servant girl new eggs are laid;
Who lays her washing by, and far and near
Goes seeking all about from day to day,
And stung with nettles tramples everywhere;
But still the cackling pullet lays away.
The boy on Sundays goes the stack to pull
In hopes to find her there, but naught is seen,
And takes his hat and thinks to find it full,
She's laid so long so many might have been.
But naught is found and all is given o'er
Till the young brood come chirping to the door.

Sweep the cat

Ann Widdecombe, MP for Maidstone and The Weald, UK

We always had animals at home, usually a cat and dog together, except for a period when we lived in Singapore. If I have to choose one to recall from childhood it has to be Monty, a smoky-coloured cat. Monty was affectionate, very intelligent and a great character. We were moving house and put him into an empty room where there was a window with two catches. Somehow, he managed to open both catches and escape. Luckily, we recovered him two days later.

In my adult life, I've had six cats – Sooty, Sweep, Pugwash the First, Carruthers, Pugwash the Second (named because Pugwash the First sadly died young at four years old), and Arbuthnot. I like to give my cats hilarious names. But it has to be Sweep, a black and white, who was my special cat. He came with Sooty, a pure black, and a flat I was buying in Fulham. Somewhat facetiously, I asked the woman who was selling up and moving to Spain whether the black cat came with the property. She said, well, yes, actually, he did. But it took her a few minutes to pluck up the courage to tell me that there was another cat that went with him.

Sweep was very round, very plump, very, very furry and agreeable. He and Sooty were with me before I became an MP and then they became Westminster cats. Sweep went on to become Ministerial. I've got a picture of him sitting on a red box. He particularly liked sleeping on social security papers but he didn't care for prison papers.

They both ate Whiskas during the week but, as this is a Catholic household, they had fish on Friday, which they loved. I'd get raw cod from my local fish and chip shop, and the Greek owners taught me the Greek words for raw fish, which I've now forgotten.

Before I became an MP, I worked regular hours and Sooty and Sweep both knew when I was coming home. Sooty would sit on the window ledge, watching people and cars come and go, and Sweep would be by the front door, sitting on the mat. A friend waiting once in my flat watched them ignore everyone and everything else and then saw how they reacted when my car pulled up.

Sweep outlived Sooty and lived to be 23 years old. I'd been getting a bit nervous about him as he'd suddenly got very thin, and I'd thought this was it. I'd had to go to Scotland for three days, and a friend looked after him. The night before I came home he'd eaten his supper and seemed fine. But when I got back, there he was, close to the mat where he used to wait for me. I knew by his body temperature that he'd only just died.

How did I feel? Obviously, abominable. But there we were in a first-floor flat, with no garden, at the height of summer. I took a taxi to the vet, with Sweep in his carrier. The driver asked if he was poorly and I said, "No, he's dead." When the time came for me to pay the fare, he wouldn't take any money.

I had Sweep cremated, like all my pets. And like them all, his ashes are in a box, stored in London. When I retire, I'll bury them all in the garden, perhaps under an apple tree.

Do I believe that my pets will be with me in an after-life? My faith teaches the opposite, that animals have no soul. I'm resigned to it but, occasionally, I do fantasise about Sooty and Sweep curled up in some celestial armchair, being fed fish by the angels.

So why do I have cats? I love them. They're delightful. They give me huge amounts of amusement, and vet bills. I wouldn't want to be without them; they're a pleasure to have around.

Although I now have a vet who'd come out at any hour of the night, it was not always so and I get very angry about the lack of a comprehensive 24-hour veterinary service. It's partly due to my own experiences over the years. Once, in the middle of the night, when Sweep was about 18, he wouldn't stop yelling and his legs were all wobbly. Our vet's surgery was on answerphone and no vet I phoned would come out except one, but he was too far away. I rang the RSPCA, who weren't interested because it was a domestic animal. Neither the Blue Cross nor the PDSA could help. The same thing happened when I lived in Fulham and saw an Alsatian knocked down in the road. A vet told me I'd have to bring the dog to him. I wondered if he'd considered the weight of such a dog, and its mood when it was injured.

It made me very angry and put me off vets for a while

because what can you do if your pet is seriously ill, you're an old lady, and it's three o'clock in the morning?

Pugwash the Second and Arbuthnot are now 10 and 11, respectively. With any luck, they will still be around when I retire to Dartmoor. It will be a very contented household. You will find it by the purrs.

La Ménagerie intime

(an extract)

Théophile Gautier
1811–1872

It is no easy task to win the friendship of a cat. He is a philosopher, sedate, tranquil, a creature of habit, a lover of decency and order. He does not bestow his regard lightly, and, though he may consent to be your companion, he will never be your slave. Even in his most affectionate moods he preserves his freedom, and refuses a servile obedience. But once gain his confidence, and he is a friend for life. He shares your hours of work, of solitude, of melancholy. He spends whole evenings on your knee, purring and dozing, content with your silence, and spurning for your sake the society of his kind.

Bud the dog, and the reptiles

Ricky Dietz, Vice President and General Curator, Audubon Zoo,
New Orleans, USA

I was born and grew up in a suburb of New Orleans, on the south-east side of the Mississippi, by a wild area behind a levee which was flooded occasionally by the river. As a boy, I was always drawn to reptiles. I collected small alligators, turtles and other amphibians to watch and learn from them before releasing them back into the wild a few hours later. One of my earliest memories is of driving down the river road with my grandfather when I was about five years old and stopping to collect toads for his garden so that they'd eat the bugs.

My parents had regular 9–5 jobs and my sister and I grew up in a household where there were always dogs. The first dog, which was my dog, was Bud, a Dalmatian, and some of my finest memories are of running and playing Frisbee with Bud on the levee. He was my confidant and I learnt from him how dogs don't judge you, they're always there for you, ever loyal come what may.

I was 24, living away from home in an apartment where pets weren't allowed, when Bud, who was 11 and staying with my mother, had to be put down. The seizures he'd begun to have had grown more frequent and serious. I felt as though I'd lost my best friend and to this day I have photos of him at home on my fridge.

As a family, we often visited the Audubon Zoo and when I was a biology student at Loyola University I worked there as a part-time volunteer for two years, shadowing the zoo-keepers, building exhibits and talking to visitors, and I spent a lot of time with the reptiles. Why do I like them? I've grown up alongside them, we've shared the same environment, and they're different, more challenging than an everyday dog or cat. You can't have the same, close relationship as you can with a dog or cat but you can get mighty fond of them, even if the feeling isn't perhaps reciprocated.

Just before I graduated, I was offered a job at the zoo and 11 years down the line, I'm now the zoo's vice president and general curator. And while I used to keep salamanders and turtles at home, now I don't, because they're here, surrounding me, all day. I'm also a stud book-keeper, working on rare breeds breeding programs with other zoos. It is exciting work. Most recently, we bred a dozen Philippine palm vipers. This is a rare, intriguing and brightly coloured secretive-natured snake which, unusually, doesn't hunt its prey but waits for its prey to come to it, thus conserving energy.

And a few years ago, in a big co-operative venture, we bred from Puerto Rican crested toads and were able to take the tadpoles to Puerto Rico where the stock was much depleted. I think that's an important role for today's zoos: breeding and conservation work, and showing people what these animals need to survive in the wild.

We have about 1300 animals in our collection and 65 staff. When it became clear that Hurricane Katrina was going to hit us, we had about 48 hours' notice and a team of 14, including two security guards and an arborealist to cut down trees, to fill containers of water for the animals to drink, get in extra food supplies, tie down or remove loose objects, and move animals inside their pens. It was definitely a hectic, dark time of long hours and deep concerns, and noise, not just from the 125 mph winds but also from the numerous helicopters flying overhead in an area that is usually a no-fly zone.

The Hurricane Team's headquarters is our reptile house. This building was chosen for several reasons: one, it is located on the highest land in the zoo. Two, it is a two-story, 16,000 square-foot brick building with only six windows. Three, it is a "building within a building", meaning there is a second concrete wall that separates the visitor side from the service area, thus creating a second "barrier" within the building's exterior brick walls. The team stays in the visitor area, secured by these two layers of walls. After the storm passes, the team sets out in pairs to inspect the facility.

The first priority was to assess the condition of the staff, mentally and physically. Next, we inspected the zoo to confirm that all the potentially dangerous animals were secured and assessed their condition. Next, we checked the status of the rest of the collection. Then we inspected the perimeter fence and made repairs to breaches where necessary. This is important to keep any loose animals in and any looters out. Upon inspection of the animals, some were found pacing nervously in their pens while others seemed to not be affected at all. Some ate willingly when offered their first meal, whereas some would not eat for several days. I did not hear a whole lot of noise as the storm passed through but I did open the door a crack to take a look but was unable to see much. The animals inside the reptile house were probably the least affected because of the aforementioned security of the building.

But as a biologist you learn quickly that animals are born and die every day, and that's the way it is. Of course, if you're a keeper, working closely with animals, then a loss can hit you a lot harder.

We were lucky we lost only four animals. A pair of young river otters who'd been removed from their usual environment and got overheated, a raccoon who ran up a tree which came down in the storm, and a young flamingo chick who I think died of fright because of the noise which distressed many animals who died of unknown circumstances. Interestingly, experience has taught us that it's better to leave outside those animals, including flamingos, whose natural environment includes hurricane and instinct tells them how to cope. Alas, the chick's natural defence mechanism hadn't developed.

We opened three months after the hurricane, on Thanksgiving Day, and we had a free weekend to show people how we'd recovered. Many of these people were locals and long-standing supporters of our zoo, who'd voted for a tax increase in the 1970s to save the zoo from closure. On those two open days in November, instead of the usual 12,000 visitors at a weekend, we had 66,000. Everyone at the zoo was working flat out – our vice presidents were taking tickets and serving burgers. It was a great occasion.

I think the experience of Katrina has taught us all lessons on how to care for animals during extreme weather conditions. Certainly, I think the New Orleans authorities are re-evaluating emergency and evacuation procedures, to take into account the needs of animals, most especially pets.

✫

MAN IS THE only animal that blushes. Or needs to.
Mark Twain 1835–1910 ✫

✫

Daisy May, Kukla and Pippen, the dogs

✫

Paula Fasseas, Banker, and Founder of PAWS, Chicago, USA

I grew up in Tucson, Arizona, in a family not the least bit interested in animals: my dad was a big hunter and as a girl, a boyfriend of my mum had presented her a dog, which was immediately given to the housekeeper.

When I was five, my godfather left a little puppy in a box by the front door. My sister and I were so excited. She was a beagle mix, so sweet and so loving. We called her Daisy May and she was supposed to live in the doghouse in the back yard but she was always in my bed. When my dad stopped by our room, Daisy May would scuttle under the bed and when he'd gone, she'd jump back up. She was very patient: I'd spend hours dressing

her in my clothes, or riding around with her in my bicycle basket. She'd travel three blocks to visit my grandparents who thought it dreadful that a dog lived inside the house and, worse, slept on my bed, but in the end, Daisy May won them over to the extent that she slept on my grandmother's bed and when she died even my dad cried.

For me, Daisy May was like my sibling and I remember lying on my bed and thinking I could spend the rest of my life with my dog and be happy. A few years before she died, when I was about 17, I found a tiny dog, a mini German Shepherd mix, in a movie theatre. She was so precious. I called her Kukla, Greek for little doll, but I couldn't take her home because I didn't want Daisy May to feel jealous, so she lived with a friend.

Three years later I got engaged to someone who'd never had anything to do with animals. We got married and moved to Chicago and my mother persuaded me against bringing the dog to Chicago, saying that I was too busy with work and Kukla was too settled. To this day, I regret that decision, that I abandoned Kukla, and wasn't there for her when she died.

When our children came along I told my husband that I couldn't have them grow up as he had done, without animals. We got two cats, Thelma and Louise, which we still have (along with three dogs, Daisy, named after my first dog, Piper and Scottie P).

One day my husband said when he saw the love the children had for these animals he realized for the first time how deprived he'd been as a child. And I think he was because animals take you to a greater depth of empathy, you learn to step outside yourself to try to understand what they need. Having animals and caring for them works magic: I've seen women prisoners locked away in maximum security behave differently, with feeling, when they have a dog in their room. And a woman with breast cancer and her young son both said how they felt comforted by the presence in their lives of a dog.

About seven months after my father died we went on holiday to Crete where my father's mother was born. We were followed everywhere by an adorable stray puppy which we fed and fussed over. I learnt that when the tourist season ends and with it the free food hand-outs, strays are poisoned by farmers to protect their chickens. I believe in karma and something inside made me think about my father dead seven months, and this dog, which was about seven months old. And then my husband said the dog had winked at him, just like my dad used to do – that did it for me and we brought the dog home and called him Pippen.

Not long after, my daughter went to do community service in an animal shelter and came back with the horrific news that in 1997 nearly 43,000 animals in Chicago were euthanased. And she said to me that if I, an animal lover, didn't do anything about it, what hope was there?

The combination of those two incidents did it for me, and I set to work. Traditional humane organizations didn't want the public to know these figures so I thought, I'll tell people. I called all my friends, the animal shelters and the media to an event where we paraded more than 100 animals and found homes for each and every one. We got 30 calls from individuals who wanted to join our organization, which at that stage didn't exist.

I set up PAWS (Pets Are Worth Saving) in 1997 and it's now the city's largest non-profit, no-kill humane organization. We want a no-kill city where no pet is destroyed simply for being homeless. To this end, we've opened a free and low-cost spey/neutering clinic in one of the most disadvantaged communities; we've an adoption centre, and we hold adoption events every weekend in local malls and banks.

Within a year of being established, we helped cut the euthanasia figures by half. Last year we performed 14,000 sterilizations, which we believe to be the way forward, and now we have several thousand volunteers aged between 18 and 70, helping at our centers, going into schools, and offering adoption advice – spreading the word. And my mother, back of the queue as an animal lover, now at the age of 84 has a rescue dog – Wawa, a terrific little Chihuahua, and my mother's conversation, which had been all about her aches and pains, is now devoted to the exploits of Wawa.

At PAWS, we hear innumerable stories of how animals have helped people: only recently, I had an email from a woman who a few years ago had adopted one of our dogs at a time when she felt her life was in ruins. The dog had died but she was writing to say that the dog she'd rescued had, in fact, rescued her.

I think that's the key to success in life – to think outside oneself and think of others. It's the guiding principle in our business life where we've set up 11 banks, all operating independently, within a community, with the aim of helping small businesses. It's the same principle in our care for animals: they do so much for us, and we do so little for them. We need to give them a voice, give them the same consideration we try to give to humans.

✿

Three Men in a Boat
– to say nothing of the dog!

(an extract)

✿

Jerome K. Jerome

1859–1927

✿

To look at Montmorency you would imagine that he was an angel sent upon the earth, for some reason withheld from mankind, in the shape of a small fox terrier. There is a sort of Oh-what-a-wicked-world-this-is-and-how-I-wish-I-could-do-something-to-make-it-better-and-nobler expression about Montmorency that has been known to bring the tears into the eyes of pious old ladies and gentlemen.

When first he came to live at my expense, I never thought I should be able to get him to stop long. I used to sit down and

look at him, as he sat on the rug and looked up at me, and think: "Oh, that dog will never live. He will be snatched up to the bright skies in a chariot, that is what will happen to him."

But, when I had paid for about a dozen chickens that he had killed; and had dragged him, growling and kicking, by the scruff of his neck, out of a hundred and fourteen street fights; and had had a dead cat brought round for my inspection by an irate female, who called me a murderer; and had been summoned by the man next door but one for having a ferocious dog at large, that had kept him pinned up in his own tool-shed, afraid to venture his nose outside the door, for over two hours on a cold night; and had learned that the gardener, unknown to myself, had won thirty shillings by backing him to kill rats against time, then I began to think that maybe they'd let him remain on earth a bit longer, after all.

To hang about a stable, and collect a gang of the most

disreputable dogs to be found in the town, and lead them out to march round the slums to fight other disreputable dogs, is Montmorency's idea of "life" . . .

☆

Victor the dog

Joan Burgess, retired civil servant, south London, UK

Victor was brought to our house by a family friend some time after he was born in July, 1941. We took one look at him and that was it. I was nine and he was given to me, but my mother, older brother and sisters all loved him. We called him Victor as it was a particularly bad time in the war, but he got

called Teddy because he looked like a cuddly bear and The Old Puppy because he was always boyish, right to the end.

When Victor was a puppy, I remember seeing my only two pairs of school uniform stockings hanging on the washing line, one with its foot savaged off. I had to go to school with a much-darned leg. But I didn't mind.

Victor had a wonderful disposition, not a bad thought in his head; he'd let you take a bone from his mouth. He had a lot of energy but he was very quiet, he'd sneeze or shake his collar to get your attention. The only time I remember him barking was just before a bomb fell quite close to our house, and he growled only when two workmen came round to mend the ceilings, which had collapsed in the blast.

Victor was one of us. He sat at the dining table on his own chair and shared our meal. He had his own plate and his own bowl (of tea), which went everywhere. At Christmas, as the youngest, I took presents out of the sack for everyone and read out the names, and we all gave Victor presents, as we did on his birthday. He'd be surrounded in wrapping paper, thoroughly enjoying himself.

He was white with black ears, a mongrel, and I think he must have had circus blood because among his tricks was the one in which he'd lie on his back and, with trembling front paws, lift a ball or a bone into the air. To this day, I don't know how he did it.

It was love of the purest kind: we wanted to be with him and he wanted to be with us. If, in the winter, he was settled comfortably by the fire, and we were all elsewhere in the house, we would hear a tiny "wuff" – i.e. *I'm too comfortable to move but I'd like somebody to come and sit with me.* Needless to say, we always hurried to oblige.

He survived for a few years after he had a big lump removed but then he started to get asthma attacks, a sign of heart failure. He'd simply worn out. We had him put to sleep just before his sixteenth birthday. My brother took him to the vet on the other side of town in a hired car. Victor loved car and train rides and my brother told us afterwards how much Victor had enjoyed that ride, looking out, interested in everything. When we all came home at the end of the day, we realised we'd left his dishes on the floor. It made us miss him terribly. Victor had a good life and, although it's 50 years since he died, not a day has gone by when I haven't thought about him. R.I.P., little lamb.

Rosie the donkey

Sara Rapoport, artist and illustrator, Surrey, UK

As well as my husband and six children, I look after Billy, the goat; Tocas, a tortoise we've had for 20 years; Oliver, an indoor cat, and Spider, a feral cat; and about 20 hens of various breeds. I didn't grow up in a particularly animal-orientated household but we always had a cat and, during the school holidays, I looked after the school rabbit and her litters. I was besotted with horses and have ridden since early childhood. And for as long as I can remember, I've wanted a field with a donkey and a goat in it, perhaps because when I was growing up, I used to pass by Dylan and Fizz who lived in a paddock not far from where we lived. From a practical point, donkeys keep the grass down and tend to be peaceable around children. They are also inexplicably appealing.

So when I heard there was a donkey for sale . . .

I didn't take to the woman on sight and Rosie was anything but a good specimen, nothing like what I'd been led to expect, but I was carried away by my desire to own a donkey. I returned with a friend who had a horsebox and handed over a cheque. On the way home, my friend echoed my concerns in no uncertain manner. She thought Rosie was older than had been claimed and that she was suffering from Cushing's disease, a pituitary problem afflicting mainly horses, which explained why she had a thick winter coat in July.

When I got home I phoned the woman, expressing my

concerns over Rosie's age and health, and she insisted I call the mobile phone number of the man from whom she'd acquired the donkey, who would verify everything she'd said, as he'd used Rosie for donkey rides on the beach.

I phoned the man but still I wasn't happy, so I contacted the Donkey Sanctuary – but on a day when their computer had crashed. I gave up. In a way, I felt Rosie was destined to stay.

She was a very gentle animal, very good-natured when children wanted a ride. She didn't bite or kick. She ambled about, not very interested in people or other animals, solitary but content. I don't for one moment think she'd been abused, more neglected. And perhaps for that reason, I never felt she bonded with me, or anyone, unless she thought we had a carrot for her.

She had a catalogue of physical woes, aside from the thick coat which had to be cropped short and expertly, to prevent lice breeding in it. Then, about three years after she'd come to us, she started to limp. The farrier showed me a pink spot in her hoof, which he diagnosed as a tumour. Both he and the vet advised having her put down. I was upset, but also relieved.

It was March. A beautiful sunny day. The friend who'd come with me to buy her arrived and Rosie looked up, probably expecting a carrot.

A van arrived and a man got out, a gun held behind his back, and walked towards us. Rosie, who'd been grazing in the field, came across quietly, willingly, and for once in many, many months, she wasn't limping. I wondered if I was imagining things.

The man went up to Rosie. He was very nice, very gentle as he talked to her and lifted the gun to her head . . . My friend forced me to turn away, urged me into the house to get the man's money. It was all over by the time I came back, and Rosie's body had been winched into the van. If I read the tone correctly, she hadn't known anything about it. But it's the part I hate: when I feel I'm playing God, deciding some animal's fate.

A gunshot is very loud and when I looked next, Billy the goat and Bonkers the sheep were at the paddock gate, staring over, puzzled, bewildered. They'd never ever stood like that before.

It wasn't like losing an animal you've had for years and which has been part of your family, but I like to think Rosie had as good a life as she could. She lived with Billy and Bonkers, and Gertie, our other goat at the time, in a field with a winter shed, near to the house, with all of us, and she could browse through the orchard or the woods, or join us in the garden. She was well fed, well groomed and very much cared for. And having her live with us has convinced me even more that I want another donkey.

Travels with a Donkey

(an extract)

Robert Louis Stevenson

1850–1894

On examination, on the morning of 4th October, Modestine was pronounced unfit for travel. She would need at least two days' repose, according to the ostler; but I was now eager to reach Alais for my letters; and, being in a civilized country of stage-coaches, I determined to sell my lady friend and be off by the diligence that afternoon. Our yesterday's march, with the testimony of the driver who had pursued us up the long hill of St Pierre, spread a favourable notion of my donkey's capabilities. Intending purchasers were aware of an unrivalled opportunity. Before ten I had an offer of twenty-five francs; and before noon, after a desperate engagement, I sold her, saddle and all, for five-and-thirty. The pecuniary gain is not obvious, but I had bought freedom into the bargain.

St Jean du Gard is a large place, and largely Protestant. The maire, a Protestant, asked me to help him in a small matter which is itself characteristic of the country. The young women of the Cevennes profit by the common religion and the difference of the language to go largely as governesses into England; and here was one, a native of Mialet, struggling with English circulars from two different agencies in London. I gave what help I could; and volunteered some advice, which struck me as being excellent.

One thing more I note. The phylloxera has ravaged the

vineyards in this neighbourhood; and in the early morning, under some chestnuts by the river, I found a party of men working with a cider-press. I could not at first make out what they were after, and asked one fellow to explain.

"Making cider," he said. "*Oui, c'est comme ça. Comme dans le nord!*"

There was a ring of sarcasm in his voice: the country was going to the devil.

It was not until I was fairly seated by the driver, and rattling through a rocky valley with dwarf olives, that I became aware of my bereavement. I had lost Modestine. Up to that moment I had thought I hated her; but now she was gone,

> And oh!
>
> The difference to me!

For twelve days we had been fast companions; we had travelled upwards of a hundred and twenty miles, crossed several respectable ridges, and jogged along with our six legs by many a rocky and many a boggy by-road. After the first day, although sometimes I was hurt and distant in manner, I still kept my patience; and as for her, poor soul! she had come to regard me as a god. She loved to eat out of my hand. She was patient, elegant in form, the colour of an ideal mouse, and inimitably small. Her faults were those of her race and sex; her virtues were her own. Farewell, and if for ever—

Father Adam wept when he sold her to me; after I had sold her in my turn, I was tempted to follow his example; and being alone with a stage-driver and four or five agreeable young men, I did not hesitate to yield to my emotion.

Donkeys, Whales & Hippopotomi

(an extract)

Reverend Jonathan Lumby

This bright morning I rose early to see my two donkeys. My path crossed a pasture wet with dew. The donkeys pushed towards me to drink and to munch carrots. I felt their warm breath. I smelt the sweetness of their coats. I stared into the wells of their eyes. Have you ever looked into a donkey's eye? Within the brown is a black circle, amazingly large, holding calm depths of mystery. The two beasts rubbed their whiskery muzzles against me. I scratched their ears, and savoured the wonder of their friendship.

Esau, a strong jackass, has lived with me since birth – for 24 years. Ruth is the other donkey. Esau loved her so much that when we moved from Somerset her owner could not bear to part Ruth and Esau. So now I have two donkeys – or they have me.

While we stood in the meadow, a thrush bounced over to see us, the warm wind sounded in the trees, and some birds sang. That's how a day should begin!

You have brought animals here to enjoy similar moments.

You respond to the grace of animals. You delight in the beauty, the friendship, the mystery of your dog, your cat, your hamster, your horse, your goat. If not, you wouldn't be here. On any day to rejoice in animals is good; on a Sunday it is particularly wonderful . . .

In these summer months I'm an adjunct to these donkeys of mine. In our villages at every fête they are fêted. Throughout hot afternoons I lead Esau and Ruth whilst youngsters balance on their backs . . . I may ask you to lead the animals while I mop my brow.

But if so, beware. You, who are used to horses will make poor leaders of donkeys. Horsey people shorten the halter-rope. They hold the rope by the beast's mouth. They tug briskly. Some pull the halter itself; they haul the animal's head from side to side. Very undignified! the donkeys think, so they refuse to budge a step. When a donkey says no, it means no.

Here's how to lead a donkey, lengthen the rope and walk well ahead, calmly. Let the donkey decide where to place its feet. Let the donkey choose when to pause and assess. Treat the animal as an equal. Give him responsibility to make up his own mind and *then,* when he is sure that you may not think it your decision but his, as a fellow-being and friend he will accompany you.

I have learnt from my donkeys, they insist on being my equals. "Does Esau belong to you?" I am asked. "I suppose so," I reply, "and I belong to him." C. S. Lewis entitled his novel *The Horse and his Boy*. Why not?

Taken from a talk Reverend Lumby gave at an Animal Service in Norfolk, UK, 1997, and used with his kind permission.

Monty the snake,
and George the cat

Paula Vickers, former science teacher, Kent, UK

We didn't keep animals at home but my father instilled in me a love of nature, and when I became a science teacher in a school in the 1970s I wanted to pass on that feeling. My lab became more like a zoo. I had rabbits, tree frogs, locusts, African land snails, a giant millipede and a snake called Monty. I wouldn't have birds because of allergies but, to help a pupil, I did house, temporarily and secretly, a chick which was turning into a cockerel. The caretaker grew suspicious but we managed to save the bird from the family cooking pot and it was rehoused by a kindly, if reluctant, aunt.

Today, health and safety rules wouldn't allow a school to keep such a menagerie but I believe a stimulating environment develops an enquiring mind and teaches children a lot about how to care for living organisms and about the cycle of life. It certainly did in one tough school where I worked. Many pupils from deprived backgrounds achieved top grades in their GCSE science exams.

Ideally, and unless they're endangered, I'd prefer animals to live in their natural environment (so now in our garden, the birds have nest-boxes, the fish are in the pond, and the ladybirds have their boxes), but sometimes it isn't possible. Years ago when I was in my early twenties, a friend bought me a rat snake. It was a gesture done with the best of intentions but by the time I was given him, Monty was over three feet long, mature and set in his live-prey eating habits, however much I tried to wean him off.

Did Monty have a character? Of course! When I removed the lid of his vivarium, he'd raise his head for me to touch his neck before I lifted him into my arms – unless he was feeling anti-social, in which case he'd just lift up his head and then retire into the box. You don't get love from a reptile, in the way you do from a cat or a dog, but I think he came to recognise the way I handled him and he'd grow twitchy hearing other people's movements across the floor. He mostly had free rein indoors and in all the years I had him, he never once tried to attack me.

You must learn about reptiles before you take one on and try to understand the environment from their perspective. You need to know when they'll defacate, and so leave them in the vivarium; that while they need heat, they must also have a cool area away from a heat mat; that if a lamp is used, it must be kept at a distance so that the animal's skin doesn't burn; that their eyes can't cope with bright sunlight; and that a large bowl of water is necessary for them to bathe in when they're ready to slough off their skin.

I made the mistake of lending Monty to an educational group and someone dropped him. I knew something was wrong when I got him back but the vet couldn't diagnose what it was. Then, one day after feeding him, I found him dead in his cage with his mouth open and a live mouse running around. I think Monty's injury had left him incapable of asphyxiating the mouse, which had then eaten its way out. I was absolutely horrified. You have to accept it as nature, the revenge of the rodent on the reptile, but I was very, very upset. I buried him in the nearby woods and shed a few tears. I vowed I'd never lend out an animal ever again.

We had a praying mantis, which was an interesting little character. My son was very fond of it and very upset when the crickets ate it while it was shedding its skin and thus was defenceless. And then there was Powerjaws, the hamster . . . But it was different losing George, our beloved cat. We'd just moved house and he escaped through an open window and got out on to the main road. The inevitable happened. I vomited with the shock and could barely talk. Cats and dogs can become really good friends, like family members, but losing them is a loss you have to learn to live with. I tell myself this many times over because I take in old cats from a sanctuary, to give them love and attention in their twilight years.

For a few years, I had my own in-house zoo – with my husband and two growing children. I like to think that I've passed on to our two children a respect for animals, nature and life, and the belief that it's a privilege to care for animals. Also, that at times, when a loved animal dies, for whatever reason, we have to cope with the emotional pain of separation and loss, and an unfounded sense of guilt.

Snake

D. H. Lawrence
1885–1930

A snake came to my water-trough
On a hot, hot day, and I in pyjamas for the heat,
To drink there.

In the deep, strange-scented shade of the great dark carob-tree
I came down the steps with my pitcher
And must wait, must stand and wait, for there he was at the
  trough before me.

He reached down from a fissure in the earth-wall in the gloom
And trailed his yellow-brown slackness soft-bellied down, over
  the edge of the stone trough
And rested his throat upon the stone bottom,
And where the water had dripped from the tap, in a small
  clearness,
He sipped with his straight mouth,
Softly drank through his straight gums, into his slack long body,
Silently.

Someone was before me at my water-trough,
And I, like a second comer, waiting.

He lifted his head from his drinking, as cattle do,
And looked at me vaguely, as drinking cattle do,
And flickered his two-forked tongue from his lips, and mused a
moment,
And stooped and drank a little more,
Being earth-brown, earth-golden from the burning bowels of
the earth
On the day of Sicilian July, with Etna smoking.

The voice of my education said to me
He must be killed,
For in Sicily the black, black snakes are innocent, the gold are
venomous.

And voices in me said, If you were a man
You would take a stick and break him now, and finish him off.

But must I confess how I liked him,
How glad I was he had come like a guest in quiet, to drink at
my water-trough
And depart peaceful, pacified, and thankless,
Into the burning bowels of this earth?

Was it cowardice, that I dared not kill him?
Was it perversity, that I longed to talk to him?
Was it humility, to feel so honoured?
I felt so honoured.

And yet those voices:
If you were not afraid, you would kill him!

• • •

And truly I was afraid, I was most afraid,
But even so, honoured still more
That he should seek my hospitality
From out the dark door of the secret earth.

He drank enough
And lifted his head, dreamily, as one who has drunken,
And flickered his tongue like a forked night on the air, so black,
Seeming to lick his lips,
And looked around like a god, unseeing, into the air,
And slowly turned his head,
And slowly, very slowly, as if thrice adream,
Proceeded to draw his slow length curving round
And climb again the broken bank of my wall-face.

And as he put his head into that dreadful hole,
And as he slowly drew up, snake-easing his shoulders, and
    entered farther,
A sort of horror, a sort of protest against his withdrawing into
    that horrid black hole,
Deliberately going into the blackness, and slowly drawing
    himself after,
Overcame me now his back was turned.

I looked round, I put down my pitcher,
I picked up a clumsy log
And threw it at the water-trough with a clatter.

I think it did not hit him,
But suddenly that part of him that was left behind convulsed in
    undignified haste,
Writhed like lightning, and was gone
Into the black hole, the earth-lipped fissure in the wall-front,
At which, in the intense still noon, I stared with fascination.

And immediately I regretted it.
I thought how paltry, how vulgar, what a mean act!
I despised myself and the voices of my accursed human
    education.

And I thought of the albatross,
And I wished he would come back, my snake.

For he seemed to me again like a king,
Like a king in exile, uncrowned in the underworld,
Now due to be crowned again.

And so, I missed my chance, with one of the lords
Of life.
And I have something to expiate;
A pettiness.

Baby the goose

Amanda Hill, holistic therapist, Somerset, UK

I had a very happy childhood, growing up with my parents, brother and two sisters in a small cottage in Wiltshire set in a four-acre garden. My parents, who were artists (graduates of the Chelsea College of Art), had moved out of London to escape the smog which had aggravated my brother's asthma. We were miles from anyone and anything and, more or less, self-sufficient and self-reliant. We had dogs and kept hens and geese, and had a huge vegetable plot, fruit trees and berry bushes. I was known to be the maternal one, and performed marriage services for our rabbits and guinea pigs, of which we had a good few. But I always wanted a goose of my own.

One day, when I was about 14, my mother, exasperated by the dozens and dozens of unhatched eggs lying about in the geese's pen, collected them all up in a box and then was distracted and left the box on a saddlestone in the garden. I came across it, picked up the eggs one by one and rattled them until I was sure I was holding one that sounded different, as though it had something inside. I popped it into my bra to keep it warm, saying nothing to anyone. I did this every day, and at night I put it in the airing cupboard inside an old nappy. I don't remember exactly how many weeks went by but one day, I heard this tap-tapping noise coming from inside my bra, followed by a loud crack. I couldn't resist taking a peek. I was so excited, I knew I had to be the first thing the goose saw if it was to be mine, and I started helping to peel away the shell.

Minutes later, there it was, soaking wet, looking up at me, and calling out with this lovely little high-pitched voice. It was instant love, of course, on my part. It was so adorable. I dried it off with the gauze lining from a nappy and called it Baby.

Baby lived in my bra during the day and slept beside me in a nappy nest on my pillow. My parents were very nonchalant about it all, seeing it as yet another example of me playing at being mother. I fed Baby grubs from the garden and special grain kept for the other baby birds, and gave him lots of water to drink. He loved water. When he was older he loved me spraying him with the hosepipe and I'm sure there was a time when he had his own paddling pool.

He grew into a fluffy yellow ball, absolutely beautiful, and I took him to school, in my pocket or a satchel. Sometimes he swam about on the fishpond, other times he sat on my lap in class. No teacher objected, and the other children were simply entranced.

Baby grew very quickly, developing great ugly feathers, some of which my father turned into quill pens. It was jolly hard the day I went back to school and had to leave him behind. I remember coming home, walking down the path, and seeing Baby running towards me at high speed, taking off at the last minute, his great wings outstretched. It was a daunting sight, quite scary. At the last moment, he tucked up his feet and folded in his wings and landed gently on my chest. As I supported his body with my arms, he wrapped his long neck round mine, and nibbled and whispered into my ear. It was like a cuddle. And that became Baby's regular welcome home for me.

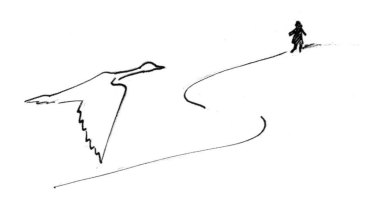

He knew my voice, and he'd come running and flying to greet me. He was greedy, like most geese, but he had a very nice nature and was incredibly gentle.

Eventually, my parents decided Baby was too big, and his droppings too large, smelly and copious, to live indoors. So he was given a pen all to himself and he seemed quite happy, living there and escaping from it when he had a mind to. He followed me everywhere and was happy rooting about as I sat nearby, reading a book.

Then my father decided he wanted to reclaim the pen to grow vegetables and Baby, who by now was about three years old, was put into the pen where the other geese lived. I think about it now and realise we wouldn't have done it if we'd known what the consequences would be. One hot day, when all the geese were in the pen, I discovered Baby in the geese's communal shed, lying alone, curled up, dead. There and then, I felt dreadful, very guilty, thinking he'd died of a broken heart, being away from me. Years later, a psychologist friend explained it to me. Baby had never thought himself to be a goose and the other geese hadn't accepted him as one. But I still don't know for sure what really happened.

We buried him in the garden and covered his grave with flowers. Baby is a big part of my memory of a happy childhood. And I like to think that he is up there, in heaven, with all the animals and people I have liked and loved and would want to see again.

☆

The law arrests . . .

Anon

☆

The law arrests the man or woman
Who steals the goose from off the common;
But lets the greater villain loose
Who steals the common from the goose.

☆

IF YOU TALK to the animals they will talk with you and you will know each other. If you do not talk to them you will not know them and what you do not know you will fear. What one fears one destroys.

Chief Dan George 1899–1981

Missy, Ophelia and Hamlet, the dogs

Adam M. Roberts, Vice President, Born Free, USA, Washington USA

I was born in Brooklyn and brought up in the Bronx by my mother on the 18th floor of a 21-story building. My maternal grandparents lived on the 10th floor and I stayed with them after school when my mother was at work. It was a world of concrete and metal and I led a lovely existence playing on the sidewalk and in the schoolyard with my friends.

When I was about 9 or 10 my mother moved to Texas into a four-bedroom house with a big yard with the man who became my step-father – which was when Missy, a German shepherd/collie cross came into my life.

Missy and I did everything together: we walked in the park or went running; we wrestled; we played Frisbee; we watched TV; and I sneaked her food from the table. Once, when I was ill, I woke up to find her licking my face and my mother said she'd been there the entire day, sitting beside me. She was a best friend, and with her my life was never lonely.

As I got to be a teenager, more energetic and out with my friends, she got older and more sedentary, and when I'd been away at college for a long while, there came a time when my parents had to have her euthanased. The shock of her loss was mitigated by the distance between us of a thousand miles and the length of time I'd had to emotionally and intellectually prepare. I'd already said my goodbyes to her when I left home.

The dogs which were The Ones in my life were Ophelia and Hamlet. I was 22 and had just moved to Washington DC in 1991 and my college girlfriend brought me this little puppy from a shelter near Vassar. It was a black Labrador crossed with husky and she fitted into my cupped hands. She was so cute, but sick with mange and roundworm. I'd studied Shakespeare and this little creature was sick and mad with her illnesses, and lovely and loving: she just had to be called Ophelia.

We got her through the maladies but when she was about five months old she developed parvo, which attacks the digestive system. The hospital said she had a 25 percent chance of recovery. I laid down my credit card and visited her every day in my lunch hour. She was in a cage, cordoned off in a room, little and listless. After three or four days, she was sitting; the following day she was standing; and the day after that I closed the door and she barked. She lived to be 14.

When Ophelia was three, I heard of a German shepherd up for adoption. In fact, he was nothing close, more Thai ridgeback or dingo. He was so muscular and a beautiful, striking red colour. He came home and fell head over heels in love with Ophelia. She'd chase a Frisbee and he'd chase her, crying because he couldn't keep up.

Within a few years he'd outgrown her, becoming a big bullish man, but he never stopped loving her. Often, he'd lie beside her, resting his head on her back.

Ophelia and Hamlet were with me when I was single and starting a life in Washington, DC, and they were my friends, my family. I remember one Thanksgiving I bought a pizza and a six-pack of beer and watched football on TV, Hamlet and Ophelia

beside me, and I was happy and quite at peace with the world in their company.

I was too nervous about their welfare to leave them in anyone's care so I took to traveling with them. I rented a car to drive with them the 1400 miles to Texas to see my mother and the 600 miles to Maine on holiday. And with a buddy, Jim, and his two dogs, we rented a mini-van to drive our dogs and us to Canada.

Then Ophelia developed arthritis, suffering periodic frightening seizures from which she recovered. But over time the attacks increased in frequency and violence until one day she had three fits in quick succession and whimpered terribly between each one. And I knew this was the time to say goodbye. I took her to the hospital that had saved her life more than a decade earlier and she was euthanased.

Despite the intense love I felt for her, it was worse losing

Hamlet. As with Missy, I'd had a chance to watch Ophelia grow old and weak and prepare myself. With Hamlet, however, one day he was fine, the next he was crippled by a cancer in his shoulder which would have meant surgery, chemotherapy, the loss of a leg, and within a short space of time death. I didn't want him to go through all that so I bade him a peaceful farewell and felt enormously empowered that I'd been given the opportunity to eliminate his terrible pain.

In college I'd seen a horrific film about a slaughterhouse. I'd never given a thought about where my food came from but from that day I became a vegetarian and decided to work in animal protection. Eventually, in 2002, I founded Born Free USA. Like our UK counterpart, we're against zoos, circuses with wild animals, trading in wild animals, and we work for animal rescue and rehabilitation and with local communities worldwide on welfare, education and conservation projects. In the US we also campaign for legislation for the estimated 15,000 primates kept in private hands and the 5,000–7,000 tigers in captivity, which is now more than are left in the wild. We work towards a goal of enabling animals to be better served and free

I'm always asked which is my favorite wild animal and the truth is I don't have one – they all touch you at some point, whether it's hearing the indri in Madagascar or seeing the bonds of friendship between orphaned elephants in an African national park. And I see this at home, whether it's my wife and step-daughter bringing home yet another waif to add to our household of dogs, cats and guinea pigs, or seeing how my three-year-old daughter is learning to care for creatures who need her to provide them with food, water, and tender care.

The pet crematorium director

Ray Hale, managing director, Cambridge Pet Crematorium,
UK and Australia

In the 1970s, when I was working for my uncle, a rag-and-bone merchant, my friend, Clive Jackman, who collected butchers' waste, lost his little Jack Russell. In those days, you took your pet to the RSPCA or the PDSA, or your vet told you to leave it with him and he'd dispose of it. Clive wasn't at all happy; he felt he'd been forced to abandon his pet, had had no time to say goodbye, and was left with a great empty space inside himself. We talked about it, talked some more, and after six months to a year of talk and research came up with the idea of opening a pet crematorium where ordinary, everyday people, like us, could bring their pet for a special or individual cremation.

I remember I was newly married, and I went home one day and told my wife, Lorna, I wanted to remortgage our house to buy a cremator. She just said, "If that's what you want to do, go ahead, I'm right behind you."

Today, our 65 members of staff at the Cambridge Pet Crematorium oversee the individual cremation of more than 25,000 pets a year. We have cremation options, a home collection service, a range of caskets and memorials, and we offer counselling. We have a beautiful seven-acre garden of remembrance where owners can scatter their pet's ashes, and on our website there is guidance on bereavement as well as the facility to post a tribute to a pet.

We spent years and years trying to make vets aware of how empty people can feel at the loss of their pet, trying to get them to address the issue of an owner's grief rather than offload it all on to a young, inexperienced veterinary nurse. I used to say to vets: if a doctor told you that your mum was dying, you wouldn't walk off and leave them to dispose of her, would you? So, why should you have to do that to your pet? Now, four times a year, with the Blue Cross Pet Bereavement Service, we hold seminars in different parts of the country, organised as a response to vets asking for training on pet bereavement.

Is all this a bit wimpy? No, I don't think so. Pets play an important part in our lives, perhaps more so in today's society where people can lead a fragmented or quite isolated life. The type of pet is immaterial: we've cremated spiders, elephants, rhinoceroses and giraffes. Whether you're young or old, rich or poor, pets are friends, companions, members of your family. I recall one man sitting in our garden of remembrance, almost inconsolable over the loss of his African parrot which hadn't left his side in more than 30 years. I've seen a distraught middle-aged woman saying goodbye to the horse she had as a 13-year-old schoolgirl.

Do you know, people keep in touch with us over the years, they pop in for a coffee if they're passing. We have thousands of appreciative letters, and we keep them all, which I think shows we're doing something which is right and necessary.

I've heard people say, "It's only a pet." I tell them they need to care for an animal to understand what loss means. I remember we had two families in, all upset except for two men, who were smirking, looking as if they didn't know why they were there. A woman in her twenties came in with the ashes of her Border collie and chose a casket which, she was advised, was three times larger than she needed. She explained that she was fulfilling an agreement. A few months before, she'd lost her husband. Before he'd died, she'd promised him she'd scatter his ashes with those of their dog on one of the walks all three had enjoyed together. The casket was for the ashes of her husband as well as her dog. I saw the expressions change on the faces of those two men. Suddenly, they understood what it was all about.

I've had pets all my life and doing this work doesn't make me immune to grief. A big part of my life was my dog, Zak. We all have a special pet. And he was it. A dog in a million. I'd lost Ben, my old German shepherd, and I went to Battersea Dogs and Cats Home to see if I could get another. I looked and looked but no dog seemed to have quite the right temperament, which was important because at the time we had three very young children. But then I turned round and saw this black German shepherd. They said he wasn't at all suitable, that he was highly nervous, having been beaten up and whipped by a previous owner. I asked to go into his cage and he let me stroke his head. As I walked out of the cage, he followed me. That was it! From then on, he seldom left my side. He came with me to work, and sat at my feet. He might've looked like the sort of dog who'd bite off your head, but many a time he'd nuzzle up to a grieving owner as if to say he was there to help them.

My wife rang me at work one day to say that Zak was ill. I rushed home and took him to the vet. His stomach had ruptured. I waited and went to see him when he was settled in his cage. He tried to get up but couldn't. He didn't make it through the night and when I got the call, I was devastated.

I went through the system at CPC, and, like everyone else, felt this yawning gap inside me. I felt absolutely terrible and cried my eyes out. It's part of the process we all have to go through. And now, when I think of him, when I look at pictures of him, I smile. I have such good memories of him. I was so lucky. He was such a character, such a fantastic dog.

Amazing, isn't it – the impact a few kilos of fur has on you? But I'm no different from anyone else.

☆

To ERR is human.
To forgive, canine.

Anon   ✿

The Power of the Dog

Rudyard Kipling

1865–1936

There is sorrow enough in the natural way
From men and women to fill our day;
And when we are certain of sorrow in store,
Why do we always arrange for more?
Brothers and sisters, I bid you beware
Of giving your heart to a dog to tear.

Buy a pup and your money will buy
Love unflinching that cannot lie –
Perfect passion and worship fed
By a kick in the ribs or a pat on the head.
Nevertheless it is hardly fair
To risk your heart for a dog to tear.

When the fourteen years which Nature permits
Are closing in asthma, or tumour, or fits,
And the vet's unspoken prescription runs
To lethal chambers or loaded guns,
Then you will find – it's your own affair, –
But . . . you've given your heart to a dog to tear.

When the body that lived at your single will,
With its whimper of welcome, is stilled (how still!),
When the spirit that answered your every mood
Is gone – wherever it goes – for good,
You will discover how much you care,
And will give your heart to a dog to tear!

We've sorrow enough in the natural way,
When it comes to burying Christian clay.
Our loves are not given, but only lent,
At compound interest of cent per cent,
Though it is not always the case, I believe,
That the longer we've kept 'em, the more do we grieve;
For, when debts are payable, right or wrong,
A short-time loan is as bad as a long –
So why in Heaven (before we are there)
Should we give our hearts to a dog to tear?

Jimmy, The Dog In My Life

(an extract)

Sir Arthur Bryant

1899–1985

Perhaps the most poignant of all memories of this beloved companion is that of the intense anxiety, and, when anxiety gave place to the knowledge that he was not to be left behind, joy with which he set out on journeys. Long before the hour of departure he would have mounted guard on the piled luggage in the hall, passionately resolute not to be left behind. Indeed, as he grew older it became quite impossible to leave home without him. And when train journeys – a far more comfortable mode of travelling with him as companion – succeeded car journeys, with what eagerness, despite old age and infirmity, did he stand in the taxi, swaying on his master's knees as it sped towards Waterloo, and with what tremendous barking, still remembered by the porters there, he entered that station, temporarily drowning every sound in the vast, echoing space but his own triumphant announcement of his coming. That so much noise could come from that minute, frail white form was something of a miracle.

I like to think that at the crack of doom I shall hear that sound again. That inseparable friend of so many years – or rather the casket containing his ashes – lies now beneath the turf of a West Country lawn looking down a valley where Dorset and Wiltshire meet and in whose woods he had often hunted rabbit, fox and badger. Gone are the sad last memories of vet and injection and the growing pain and infirmity of those last years – so bravely and patiently borne. There only remains the recollection of an unquenchable vitality and capacity for life, above all for love and loyalty, and of something which for want of a better

word I can only call nobility. True to his nature as a dog – fierce, independent, proud and predatory – he displayed towards the humans who befriended him a trust, a selfless tenderness and devotion that nothing could alter and which as much as any experience of life, has convinced me that, in some mysterious way beyond our understanding, love is eternal.

✧

The pet bereavement counsellor
✧

Jo-Ann Dono, head, the Pet Bereavement Support Service, and director, SCAS, Oxfordshire, UK

✧

The Pet Bereavement Support Service is a service set up in 1994 by SCAS (the Society for Companion Animal Studies), after research showed there was no real support for people suffering bereavement at the loss of a pet. It began as a helpline, manned by volunteers, and from the outset grew tremendously. In fact, to such an extent that five years later, and in partnership with The Blue Cross, a lottery grant enabled the service to go national.

We now have a freephone helpline (8.30 am to 8.30 pm every day of the week), manned by co-ordinators who can direct a caller to one of 90 befrienders nationwide. An email service was launched a few years ago which provides another support option for pet owners.

It takes a lot of courage for someone who has lost their pet to make that first phone call. They can be in huge distress and yet, sometimes, three to five minutes talking to a co-ordinator can be enough. If it isn't, a caller is given the first name, phone number and hours worked by the befriender nearest to them.

Many of our befrienders work full-time, a number in the housing sector or with elderly people; some are at home with children. We try to create opportunities for people with mobility problems or, indeed, whatever someone's circumstance. A befriender must commit to a minimum of six hours a week to take calls in their own home, after completing a correspondence training course over a period of between four and six months.

A befriender is different from a formally trained counsellor who is an "external" expert. A befriender is a listening ear, offering reassurance that a great sense of loss is normal and understandable, and is not a sign of madness.

The initial contact call to a befriender lasts usually about 40 to 45 minutes and the caller is given the option to call back which they do, on average, two or three times. That said, some people ring back once simply to say thank you, others to say that they've got another pet. Of course, there are people who take six months or longer to heal and there are some you realise will carry their grief for the rest of their life. And, yes, some people's problems aren't solely to do with the loss of their pet – they have their own life issues – and our befrienders have details of other more appropriate organisations which the caller might wish to contact.

People can feel guilty about taking the life of something they love, wondering if they could or should have done things differently. But it's a question of responsibility and quality of life. You are the animal's carer, and the animal is looking to you to do the best you can for it.

The loss of a young animal or an unexpected loss due to something such as a road traffic accident can cause a lot of shock and despair, and self-questioning about whether the death could have been prevented. And for people whose pet has gone missing, coming to terms with a loss when there is no body is also not easy.

Why do we grieve for a lost pet? There are as many different reasons as there are people. Pets tend to be always there, a constant in your life, and when they die, you realise how much you miss them. You sense the gap and raw emotion of loss. And the bond can be a pure, uncomplicated form of affection, of love. Dana, my Labrador, sitting happily at my feet, is nine. I've had her since she was six weeks old and I bring her into work every day. We're inseparable and my

family have told me that they don't want to be around me when she goes.

I grew up in a dog-and-cat household, with the occasional hamsters, rabbits and birds, and now I'm a trained psychologist, with experience in counselling, social psychology and academia, but that doesn't stop me grieving when one of my pets dies. But my knowledge helps me understand that it's perfectly normal to feel I've suffered a big loss, and that this awful feeling will come to an end.

I think it helps to be prepared so I'd recommend that an owner recognises that their pet is more likely to die before they do and, with that in mind, they enjoy the time they spend with their pet. As the pet gets older, they should think about its life ending and, if they have the choice, how and where they'd want it done. I'd advise discussing the options with a vet. There are many more choices, including cremation or home burial, than there were 10 to 15 years ago. It can also be helpful to take on a younger animal as your pet gets older. Very often this can give an older pet a new lease of life and it can also help the owner with the grieving process when the older pet dies.

Last year, I lost my cat Pushkin, a part Burmese, after a long struggle with cancer. I was absolutely shattered and then suddenly, months down the line, I decided to take in two Burmese kittens. They're a lot of work, my "posh" cats, as I call them, but I think of them as a tribute to Pushkin and I'm enjoying the energy and lightness they bring into my home, and I'm enjoying reinvesting my love in two other animals. It's what our befrienders tell every caller: most people recover sufficiently to get another animal. It's not right for everyone, but it was certainly right for me.

☆

Elvis, Jesus and Coca-Cola

(an extract)

☆

Kinky Friedman   ☆

On January 4, 1993, the cat in this book, and the books that preceded it, was put to sleep in Kerrivale, Texas by Dr W. H. Hoegemeyer and myself. Cuddles was fourteen years old, a respectable age. She was as close to me as any human being I have ever known.

Cuddles and I spent many years together, both in New York, where I first found her as a little kitten on the streets of Chinatown, and later on the ranch in Texas. She was always with me, on the table, on the bed, by the fireplace, beside the typewriter, on top of my suitcase when I returned from a trip.

I dug Cuddles' grave with a silver spade, in the little garden by the stream behind the old green trailer where both of us lived in summertime. Her burial shroud was my old New York sweatshirt and in the grave with her is a can of tuna and a cigar.

A few days ago I received a sympathy note from Bill Hoegemeyer, the veterinarian. It opened with a verse by Irving Townsend: "We who choose to surround ourselves with lives even more temporary than our own live within a fragile circle . . ."

Now, as I write this, on a gray winter day by the fireside, I can almost feel her light tread, moving from my head and my heart down through my fingertips to the keys of the typewriter. People may surprise you with unexpected kindness. Dogs have a depth of loyalty that often we seem unworthy of. But the love of a cat is a blessing, a privilege in this world.

They say when you die and go to heaven all the dogs and cats you've ever had in your life come running to meet you.

Until that day, rest in peace Cuddles.

☆

Tasha, Judy, Minah, Gyp, Tessa, Freddie, Kizzy, Louie, Charlie and ☆ Millie, the dogs

Jenny Seagrove, actress and animal rights activist, London, UK

I was born and brought up in Malaysia and was lucky to play with orphaned baby bears and orang-utans who were adopted and cared for by a friend, in the days before such animals would be carted off to zoos. My mother, in particular, was an animal lover and at one time my brother and I had two rabbits, Mug and Sooty, which were thought to be brothers. Not long after we found we had 41 baby rabbits.

And we had dogs. The first one I remember was Judy, a black, even-tempered, gorgeous mongrel who I adored and who, one day, when I was about seven, walked into the jungle to die. Even at that age, I understood that was what she wanted to do, to be private and alone, but I was heartbroken.

We had Minah, a cocker spaniel, and then Gyp, an Oscar Wilde of a dog – chilled but great style. He was a handsome gentleman, with a white cross on his chest, white paws, tan eyebrows and a black curly tail. When the car came down the driveway, I could hear him singing.

I was sent back to England to boarding school so I saw the dogs only once a year. I missed them dreadfully and when they died while I was away at school I was devastated not to be there with them. There was Tessa, or Slitty, because her eyes would close up if she thought we were cross with her. There was Sally and a Dalmatian I didn't get to know because I'd left home.

I had about three dogless years while I was at drama school but when my disabled mother returned from Malaysia to live in Sussex I set about finding her a dog as a companion. I thought a small dog would suit her and when I was introduced to this quiet runt of a cocker spaniel sitting in silence under a table, staring back at me . . .

We called her Natasha, or Tasha, the heroine in *War and Peace*, which I was reading, and it wasn't many months before she came to live with me because my mother couldn't cope with her energetic needs. I wasn't sure if I could cope any better. I was young and embarking on a career as an actress, not the most routine of lifestyles, and living in a small flat London. It turned out much better than I expected. Tasha was a well-behaved girl and when I got work I was able to take her to rehearsals, popping out in any break times to take her for a walk. There'd be occasions when I had to leave her for the day and I saw that she wouldn't touch her food until I got home.

Tasha and I were together for more than 15 years. We grew up together and she was my soul mate. I can't say why but we were tuned in to one another. I was upset one day and crying and she came to sit quietly beside me and lick my face. She was very special, and knowing. And I'm quite sure she saved me from being raped. We were walking one day along a deserted country road. There was a lone, parked car and I felt very uneasy and uncomfortable. A man appeared, with his shirt open and adrift, and Tasha went mental, absolutely mental. The man walked by and said, "Shame about the dog," and when I glanced back, he was exposing himself. I believe I had a very lucky escape. Thanks to Tasha.

I feel bad that I kept Tasha too long, that she'd been ready to go off into the jungle, as it were, knowing it was her time to die. Her legs had gone and for six months I wheeled her round in a pram to take her to the park. But then there came a day . . .

she had a walk, a meal and a trip in the car which she loved. Then the vet came, shaved her leg and gave her an injection. She went really quickly and it was so peaceful, as though she was perfectly ready, perfectly prepared . . . And I knew then that I'd held on to her, incapable of letting her go because I loved her and needed her so much. I regret that to this day.

After she'd died, people told me that she was still with me, still around me in some way. I felt it, too. But I have never, ever felt in such a black pit of despair, and grief that seemed to go on and on and on. I found books that helped me through, which made me feel I was not alone.

You say "never again" but some 18 months later we took in Freddie. He'd been re-homed four times and we were his last hope. But he bit three people within as many days, including me who he adored, and the vet said he was full of so much rage – which is caused by cocker spaniel in-breeding – that it'd be kinder to have him put to sleep. That was a terrible, terrible thing to experience – to have a young and otherwise healthy dog for a week and then watch him being put to sleep.

Then came Kizzy, a rescue girl who'd probably suffered abuse. She was a stubborn, wilful girl. And I loved her to bits. When she grew sick and was misdiagnosed, I did everything I could to help her, forcing her to eat when she was past it. And then a second vet diagnosed an incurable, inoperable cancer. After she was put to sleep and before I could give her up, I held her in my arms for four hours.

It was only a week later a pet sanctuary rang to say there was a springer spaniel in desperate need of a home. He was as thin as a rake, had open wounds on his paws from the concrete floors, and his eyes were out on stalks. That's how we came away with Louie.

He came to live with us and for two years he was best mates with Charlie, an old Labrador/Doberman cross, the dog of a frail elderly friend, who'd come to live with us. When Charlie died, Louie was devastated. A week later, when we were in the thick snow of a cold winter, a couple approached us. They'd rescued a nine-year-old Jack Russell cross from a life of living outdoors. "He's so sweet," they said. And then those fatal words, "Just come and take a look."

Millie smiled at me and I smiled back. And that was it. Louie ignored her but my partner, Bill, just didn't connect with her at all. We hummed and we ha'd. And then we all got in the car. I was driving. Bill fell asleep. Millie climbed on to his chest, and fell asleep. They both snored. Louie didn't take any notice. And now Louie and Millie are the best of friends and Bill thinks Millie is the most beautiful of dogs.

Nowadays I'm known as much for being an animal rights activist and a vegetarian as an actress. I think this has come about because of being brought up with animals and, over years, seeing how animals suffer at the hand of man. An animal has no voice, very few rights and those are only what we choose to give them. I feel it's getting worse; equally, I feel it's my duty to do what I can to help.

I'm not a religious person but I do feel there's a greater energy, a universal force, and that there are many different layers of existence and that, in some way, this is where our energy goes. Which is why I think we might encounter, if not meet up with, our much-loved pets.

KINDNESS TO ALL God's creatures is an absolute essential rock-bottom necessity in any world where peace and righteousness are to prevail.

William Grenfell 1865–1940

Gimmy the dog

Selladurdi Ragunathan, electrical engineer and businessman, south London, UK

I was born and brought up in Sri Lanka, a few miles from Trincomalee, one of the biggest natural harbours in the world on a coastline of long white beaches and mangrove lagoons. My father worked for the RAF and then the Sri Lankan air force, and my mother was a housewife. I was the youngest of three brothers and a sister and dogs were always about in my house, but there was one only who was special to me. He was called Gimmy. He was a great big grey and white dog, a very hairy dog, with hair covering his face.

I was six when he arrived at our house and right from the start we became friends. He was my constant companion and playmate. And whenever I was reprimanded by my mother, I sought him out. He'd wait for me if I played football or we'd just sit together and I'd talk to him about this or that. We swam together in the big lake close to our house and if ever I was

lagging behind Gimmy would swim back to me, and wait for me to catch my breath before we'd swim on. If someone had asked me if I had a best friend I'd have said, "No, I have a best dog."

In those days, dogs weren't treated as pets and, for reasons of hygiene, they weren't allowed to sleep inside the house. They weren't fussed over, there weren't tins of special dog food; dogs ate what we ate. During mealtimes Gimmy sat by me. Never once did he beg for food or grab at something; he'd wait until he was served – rice and stock from a curry, and some bones. Sometimes I'd give him my meal.

He was a large dog and people were frightened of the way he looked. In fact, he looked a sleepy, lazy dog and he was very easy going. But if any visitor raised his voice to anyone in the family, or looked as if they were about to be naughty or possibly steal something, Gimmy would lift his head and give them a look. That look would stop them in their tracks.

Gimmy would wait on the verandah for the last person in the family to return home and only then would he settle down at night. And in all the time I played with him, he never once lost his temper with me. But I do remember my father got into an argument with some fellow outside the house and Gimmy ran and jumped over the wall and took hold of the fellow's neck. Word soon got round that we had a dangerous dog, which was a force *not* to be reckoned with.

I was 12 when we suffered an especially heavy cyclone. We had to move out of the house to a safer area. We called to Gimmy to follow us, which, unusually, he didn't. I put a lead on him and tried to drag him off the verandah but he wouldn't budge. Eventually, we decided we had to leave him. When we returned, our big old house was razed to the ground. My father was convinced that Gimmy was alive and well somewhere in the debris. We searched and searched and then we found his body buried under the wall where he had taken shelter against the wind and the rain.

I was ill with grief. I dreamt about him, I'd go looking for him. I wept a great deal.

My father buried him under the lemon trees and friends and family came to sit with us as we mourned, remembering him and what a special dog he was. We took flowers to his grave and I took him food.

Gimmy gave me real love, which I shall never forget. And every time I see a dog, from that day to this, I think of him. You could have all the money in the world but it doesn't mean you could find a dog like Gimmy.

SOMETIMES HE SITS at your feet looking into your face with an expression so gentle and caressing that the depth of his gaze startles you. Who can believe that there is no soul behind those luminous eyes?

Théophile Gautier 1811–1872

Dinah in Heaven

Rudyard Kipling
1865–1936

She did not know that she was dead,
But, when the pang was o'er,
Sat down to wait her Master's tread
Upon the Golden Floor,

With ears full-cock and anxious eyes,
Impatiently resigned;
But ignorant that Paradise
Did not admit her kind.

Persons with Haloes, Harps and Wings
Assembled and reproved,
Or talked to her of Heavenly things,
But Dinah never moved.

There was one step along the Stair
That led to Heaven's Gate;
And, till she heard it, her affair
Was – she explained – to wait.

And she explained with flattened ear,
Bared lip and milky tooth—
Storming against Ithuriel's Spear
That only proved her truth!

Sudden – far down the Bridge of Ghosts
That anxious spirits clomb—
She caught that step in all the hosts,
And knew that he had come.

She left them wondering what to do,
But not a doubt had she.
Swifter than her own squeals she flew
Across the Glassy Sea;

Flushing the Cherubs everywhere,
And skidding as she ran,
She refuged under Peter's Chair
And waited for her man.

• • •

There spoke a Spirit out of the press,
Said: – "Have you any here
That saved a fool from drunkenness,
And a coward from his fear?

"That turned a soul from dark to day
When other help was vain?
That snatched it from wan hope and made
A cur a man again?"

"Enter and look," said Peter then,
And set The Gate ajar.
"If I know aught of women and men
I trow she is not far."

"Neither by virtue, speech nor art
Nor hope of grace to win;
But godless innocence of heart
That never heard of sin:

"Neither by beauty nor belief
Nor white example shown.
Something a wanton – more a thief –
But – most of all – mine own."

"Enter and look," said Peter then,
"And send you well to speed;
But, for all that I know of women and men
Your riddle is hard to read."

Then flew Dinah from under the Chair,
Into his arms she flew –
And licked his face from chin to hair
And Peter passed them through!

> You THINK THOSE dogs will not be in Heaven? I tell you, they
> will be there long before any of us.
>
> *Robert Louis Stevenson 1850–1894*

Smokey the dog

Warren Eckstein, author, broadcaster, pet and animal expert,
California, USA

I grew up in a typical Jewish family, which moved from the Bronx to Long Island, New York and where there were always 15–20 people somewhere about in the house. I didn't feel comfortable with it and when I was about seven or eight I'd take off to the creek behind the house and hang out with the ducks, the rats, rabbits and beavers. I felt more comfortable talking to them than with the upright beings indoors. And over the years it's true to say I've had more problems relating to uprights than ever I have with animals.

I was about 10 when my parents bought a dog from Macy's in New York, which at that time had a pet department. In those days people chose their dogs because of two popular TV programs: they were either *Rin Tin Tin* fans and bought German shepherds or *Lassie* fans and bought collies. I'm a *Rin Tin Tin* man and my parents got a German shepherd who we called Smokey.

Old schoolfriends remember her fondly to this day, especially the several whose butts she bit. Not because she was a bad-tempered, snappy dog but because she was playful and we were playful boys. So I smile when I imagine these old friends with four tiny decades-old puncture wounds on their rear ends.

My parents had the kind of love for animals that allowed them to be themselves, and I learnt from that. So, if Smokey wanted to dig a hole in the back yard, Smokey got to dig a hole in the back yard. If Smokey wanted to bark at a squirrel, Smokey got to bark at a squirrel. That's what dogs did and so that's what Smokey got to do. She was allowed to be a dog; she was not micro-managed as many animals are, alas, today. When I go into a house and say to a dog, "Sit!" and the dog gives me that challenging look that says, *You talking to me, Warren?*, I'm happy this is a dog, not a micro-managed animal.

I'm not against discipline but I am anti the Gestapo training that insists animals behave in a certain way. I remember someone who was against dogs sniffing other dogs' butts in the park. "Look!" I said. "This is the doggy equivalent of surfing! It's Yahoo-ing, Google-ing or whatever for dogs!"

I train with love, through hugs and kisses. There were 200 disturbed, aggressive Chihuahuas rescued from a home which a judge had ordered be put down. I rehabilitated them all to the extent the judge reprieved them and now all are happily rehoused, including Cisco, who came to live with us, and Skyler, another German shepherd rescue.

I was in my late teens when Smokey died of natural causes in her sleep. She'd got to be an old dog, which doesn't stop the grieving but there is then also a sense of relief and release that an animal is no longer in pain, no longer suffering.

I keep her collar in the night-table next to my bed. And,

yes, I take it out from time to time and do that thing that all people do who've loved and lost a beloved animal – I cry and I laugh as I recall this dog that didn't need me to perform, that accepted me for what I was, a crazy, emotional kid who kissed and cuddled her. Yes, I cry and laugh as I remember the dog who was my best friend.

I used to live in a farmhouse dating from 1802 with my wife, Fay, and our rescue animals – 15 dogs, six chickens, six ducks, 30 cats and two great big pigs, Corky and Spotty, who happily came jogging with me. When Fay died young, at 36, after 19 years of marriage and within six months of being diagnosed, an amazing thing happened. The animals grieved, even the chickens. How do I know? Their behavior was different, their sleeping, eating habits altered. The dogs, cats and pigs especially seemed to go through the textbook four stages of grief – anger, depression, anxiety and guilt. People seem to forget or not even realize that animals are emotional creatures. And because I found myself helping the animals through their grief, dealing with my own grief was delayed, to the point I was ready to deal with it.

I was living back east after Fay died and I'd come to Los Angeles to do a radio program. Publicity photos were needed of me with a dog but I didn't have one to hand. By chance, someone in the team knew a lovely woman who'd adopted Rio, a German shepherd, from a rescue centre in Seattle. We drove across country, had the pictures taken and the lovely woman, Denise, and I have been together now for 15 years. We lost Rio about six years ago and I had a large portrait of him tattooed on my right leg which is the side he liked to walk on. So he's with me always.

I'm not a very religious person but I do believe there's a heaven where we'll meet up with our animals. They must be there, mustn't they, if you compare who sins more – animals or people? Which is God going to choose? And if they're not there, I'll hang out with them in hell.

☆

If It Should Be

Anon

☆

If it be I grow frail and weak,
 And pain should wake me from my sleep,
Then you must do what must be done,
For this last battle can't be won.
You will be sad, I understand,
Don't let your grief then stay your hand,
For this day more than all the rest,

Your love and friendship stand the test.
We've had so many happy years,
What is to come will hold no fears,
You'll not want me to suffer, so,
When the time comes, please let me go.
I know in time you too will see,
It is kindness you do me,
Although my tail its last has waved,
From pain and suffering I've been saved.
Do not grieve that it should be you,
Who has to decide this thing to do
We've been so close, we two, these years,
Don't let your heart hold any tears.

Bob the dog, and Brains the cat

Susie Cornfield, *writer and publisher, south London, UK*

I grew up with an Alsatian cross, rescued from Battersea Dogs and Cats Home. I'm an only child and for 10 years Bob was my greatest friend. My mother says that when I was a baby she watched dumbstruck from the top of the house as Bob saw off what she took to be a potential kidnapper creeping up on my pram in the back garden.

When I was a toddler Bob patiently let me dress him in baby clothes and, when measles and chickenpox confined me to a darkened bedroom, he stayed with me throughout a long, tedious summer.

Wherever we went, Bob came too, until family circumstances removed him to live with Auntie Sylvia in Liverpool, hundreds of miles away. It was supposedly a temporary measure but Bob never came home. My mother said he'd settled in too well to be moved again. The last I saw of him, he was staring out of a newspaper, in an advert for the anti-vivisection society which had approached my aunt in the street, asking for a photograph of his wise old, sad old eyes. I missed him but was proud of him, and chuffed that someone else had also seen how special he was.

Years went by, with long working hours and no animals, and then, during a prolonged, mostly horizontal bout of back problems, a friend recommended getting a cat. A cat? No self-respecting dog person has a cat. Besides which, cats'd have your eyes out, soon as look at you. No, no, no . . .

Which is when Brains came into my life.

One vaguely upright evening, two ladies from Cats Protection arrived with several cages. My friend was there because, although I'd researched the subject of cat-care, I was doubtful. Not to say scared. I was interviewed about my cat-experience and cat-commitment and then the first cage was opened. A tall, skinny, black and white creature strode purposefully across the room towards me, jumped on to my lap and settled there without giving me a second look. I was hooked. And remained so for the 16 years we were together.

Until the end, Brains was at the door to welcome me home, and at the door to follow me if I went out, so, I took to driving round the corner, out of sight, before continuing journeys on foot. She'd wait out in all weathers, complaining vociferously to neighbours who consequently came to know my every movement.

Brains was vocal and I'm sure had perfect pitch. She complained bitterly when I attempted to learn the piano but sat contentedly under the piano stool when a young, accomplished friend came round to play. I took to learning the flute and in the early days, Brains would yowl and tap the end of the instrument, as if trying to get me to stop causing this thing any more pain.

For years, she was hostile to visitors, excepting two – Sara, this book's illustrator, and another confirmed cat-aholic – and would slam out of the cat-flap until they'd left, although she did grow to enjoy keeping a close eye on whatever any workman was up to.

She detested the new kitten, which arrived in the house in her middle age but, outside, she'd defend him from two big bullying cats, putting her own safety at risk. She'd sit with me in the bathroom when I was ill, putting a paw on my hand, and when I went horizontal again for weeks, she lay on the bed, one regular visitor asking if she'd been stuffed.

A kind neighbour who cared for Brains while we were away on holiday held the phone to her ear when I called. Brains' ears pricked up. She recognised my voice and we conversed. What? Yes, of course, I'd left her a map with our journey and itinerary dates, etc., and sent her postcards, but I had to call, didn't I? To put her mind at rest.

Brains would've followed me to the ends of the earth and when she died – two operations having failed to remove a virulent cancer – amidst the guilt (should we have had her put to sleep earlier to prevent the misery she went through?), amidst the shock and wretchedness at losing a companion of many years, I realised that this was the first journey she'd made without me.

Why was she named Brains? Because she was tall, skinny, attractive and, well, different from other cats I'd met, characteristics which, for some reason, reminded me of the American actress, Katharine Hepburn. I knew I didn't want to stand in the street calling out, "Fish, Katharine Hepburn, come get your fish!", so I thought about what made Miss Hepburn different from many other actresses of her day. It was easy. So, Brains it was.

If Brains were here now she'd be sitting on this desk beside me as I write, as she was beside me in the good times and those times of despair we all endure. I feel immensely privileged to have loved and cared for so singular a creature and, while I have no idea if there is a heaven, I only know that for me, there can't be one if Brains, my MagnifiCat, isn't there beside me. Farewell, my Lovely.

Last Words to a Dumb Friend

Thomas Hardy

1840–1928

Pet was never mourned as you,
Purrer of the spotless hue,
Plumy tail, and wistful gaze,
While you humoured our queer ways,
Or outshrilled your morning call
Up the stairs and through the hall –
Foot suspended in its fall –
While, expectant, you would stand
Arched, to meet the stroking hand,
Till your way you chose to wend
Yonder, to your tragic end.

Never another pet for me!
Let your place all vacant be;
Better blankness day by day
Than companion torn away.
Better bid his memory fade
Better blot each mark he made
Selfishly escape distress
By contrived forgetfulness,
Than preserve his prints to make
Every morn and eve an ache.

From the chair wheron he sat
Sweep his fur, nor wince thereat;
Rake his little pathways out
Mid the bushes roundabout;
Smooth away his talons' mark
From the claw-worn pine-tree bark,
Where he climbed as dusk enbrowned
Waiting us who loitered round.

Strange it is this speechless thing,
Subject to our mastering,
Subject for his life and food
To our gift, and time, and mood;
Timid pensioner of us Powers
His existence ruled by ours
Should by crossing at a breath
Into safe and shielded death,
By the merely taking hence
Of his insignificance –
Loom as largened to the sense,
Shape as part, above man's will
Of the Imperturbable . . .

Prayer for Gentleness
to all Creatures

John Galsworthy
1867–1933

To all the humble beasts there be,
To all the birds on land and sea,
Great Spirit, sweet protection give
That free and happy they may live!

And to our hearts the rapture bring
Of love for every living thing;
Make us all one kin, and bless
Our ways with Christ's own gentleness!

Bibliography

The publisher is grateful for permission to reproduce the following extracts (in order of appearance):

'Alligator/Crocodile' by Mary Ann Hoberman. Reprinted by permission of The Gina Maccoby Literary Agency. Copyright © 1973, renewed 2001 by Mary Ann Hoberman.

'Song of the Battery Hen' by Edwin Brock. Reprinted with permission of Mrs Elizabeth Brock and David Higham Associates Ltd.

'Reflections' by Virgina McKenna. Reprinted with kind permission of Miss McKenna, co-founder in 1984 with her late husband Bill Travers and eldest son Will of Zoo Check, which became the Born Free Foundation on whose website – www.bornfree.org.uk – this poem resides.

'Dog's Death' from *Collected Poems 1953–1993* by John Updike, copyright © 1993 by John Updike. Used by permission of Alfred A. Knopf, a division of Random House, Inc.

'Fish'n'dips' by B.B. Edwards, copyright ©2009 by Susie Cornfield, and used with her permission.

Captain Corelli's Mandolin by Louis de Bernières, published by Vintage (May 1995). Extract reprinted by permission of The Random House Group Ltd.

On A Clear Day (Michael O'Mara Books Limited, 1995), extract from his autobiography used by permission of David Blunkett.

'Wishful thinking' by Susie Cornfield, copyright ©1995 by Susie Cornfield and used with her permission.

Chewing the Cud by Dick King-Smith (2001), extract used by permission of A.P. Watt Ltd on behalf of Fox Busters Ltd.

'Verse for a Certain Dog' by Dorothy Parker, reproduced by permission of Pollinger Ltd and The National Association for the Advancement of Coloured People.

War Horse by Michael Morpurgo. Text © Michael Morpurgo 1982. Published by Egmont UK Ltd, and extract used with their permission.

Jimmy, The Dog In My Life by Arthur Bryant (Lutterworth Press, 1960), extract used by permission of David Higham Associates Limited.

The publisher acknowledges and recommends to interested readers these collections and works in which the following poems, sayings and prose were discovered:

'The Dead Sparrow' by William Cartwright in *Come Hither*, Walter de la Mare (Puffin Books, 1957)

'The Power of the Dog' and 'Four-Feet', from *Collected Dog Stories* by Rudyard Kipling (Macmillan, 1934).

La Ménagerie intime, an extract, by Théophile Gautier in *The Enchanted Cat*, John Richard Stephens (Prima Publishing & Communications, California, USA, 1990)

'A Farmer's Boy', Anon; 'Epitaph on a Hare' by William Cowper; 'Baby Tortoise', an extract, by D. H. Lawrence in *Pet Poems*, Robert Fisher (Faber and Faber Ltd, 1989)

'Snake' by D. H. Lawrence (*Contemporary Verse*, Longmans, 1949 and *The Nation's Favourite Animal Poems*, BBC Worldwide Limited, 2001)

'Little Paws', Anon, in *Bless All Thy Creatures, Lord*, Richard Newman (Macmillan Publishing Co Inc., Collier Macmillan Canada, Inc., 1982)

'Prayer for Gentleness to all Creatures' by John Galsworthy; 'Stray goat' by Elizabeth Montagu; 'The Trap' by E. G. C. Beckwith; 'The Dog' by Jerome K. Jerome; 'Heaven' by Rupert Brooke; 'Prayer of a Horse' by Maurice Portal; 'An Epitaph' by Lord Byron in *The Neighbours*, Fougasse (The Universities Federation for Animal Welfare, 1954)

'Lonely House', Anon; 'If It Should Be', Anon; 'Requiem for Pluto', Anon; 'If God had wanted a Gerbil', Anon; 'Last Words to a Dumb Friend' by Thomas Hardy in *Goodbye, Dear Friend* by Virginia Ironside (Robson Books, 1994)

'Hen's Nest' by John Clare, found on a website and confirmed by the John Clare Society as being in *Bird Poems* (Folio Society, 1980)

'The law arrests . . .' Anon, found on the web, along with other works.

Useful information – not exhaustive

(in chronological order)

Averil Jarvis MBE

is the founder of The Cinnamon Trust

10 Market Square, Hayle, Cornwall TR27 4HE, UK

www.cinnamon.org.uk

National charity, founded in 1985 by Mrs Jarvis, to help the elderly and
terminally ill care for their pets in the short and long term.

Brian Fisher

works at the California Academy of Sciences

55 Music Concourse Drive, Golden Gate Park,

San Francisco CA 94118, USA

www.calacademy.org

Exploring, explaining and protecting the natural world. Since 1853.

Paul Klusman

stars with his cats in . . .

www.youtube.com/watch?v=mHXBL6bzAR4

Stanley Smith

worked at Serenity Park, Horticultural Therapy Program for the
Association for Parrot C.A.R.E. PO Box 84042,

Los Angeles, CA 90073, USA

www.parrotcare.org/index.html

A green secluded area, offering ecotherapy to traumatised US veterans and
damaged birds.

Kay, Duchess of Hamilton

works for Advocates for Animals

10 Queensferry Road, Edinburgh, Scotland EH2 4PG, UK

www.advocatesforanimals.org.uk

Advocates for Animals is Scotland's leading animal protection organisation, working for animals through high-profile campaigns, political lobbying, investigations and public education.

Brigitte Bardot
is the founder of the Fondation Brigitte Bardot
28 rue Vineuse 75116 Paris, France
www.fondationbrigittebardot.fr
Founded in 1986, the organisation works worldwide, in the field and in courts of law, for pet and animal protection.

Trevor Knight
supports Orang-utan Appeal UK
11 Forest Hall, Brockenhurst, New Forest, Hampshire, SO42 7QQ, UK
www.orangutan-appeal.org.uk
Dedicated to the rehabilitation and preservation of orang-utans and their habitat.

Mark Habben
works for London Zoo
Regent's Park, London NW1 4RY, UK
www.londonzoo.co.uk
The world's first scientific zoo opened in 1828 and is now part of the Zoological Society of London, a charity dedicated to the wordwide conservation of animals and their habitats, and to education.

Jilly Cooper
is a well-known author and animal lover
www.jillycooper.co.uk

Tony Bridgefoot
owns Bluebell Lakes
Tansor, Oundle, Peterborough, Cambridgeshire PE8 5HP, UK
www.bluebell-lakes.co.uk
Six fishing lakes and a lot of big carp.

Peter Chege
works for The Brooke
30 Farringdon Street, London, EC4A 4HH, UK
www.thebrooke.org
Helping working horses, donkeys and mules in the world's poorest communities.

Dr Irene Pepperberg
is the author of *Alex & Me, How a Scientist and a Parrot Uncovered a Hidden World of Animal Intelligence – and Formed a Deep Bond in the Process* (HarperCollins).

Diana Eccleston
worked for The Royal Society for the Prevention of Cruelty to Animals (the RSPCA)
Wilberforce Way, Southwater, Horsham, West Sussex RH13 9RS, UK
www.rspca
Since 1824 the RSPCA has worked to promote kindness and prevent cruelty to animals, its inspectors working round the clock to save animals in distress.

Mary Black
works for Battersea Dogs and Cats Home
4 Battersea Park Road, London SW8 4AA, UK
www.battersea.org.uk
Rescuing lost and unwanted dogs since 1860 and cats since 1883, and devoted to reuniting animals with their owners or finding them loving, permanent new homes.

James Barnett
works as vet consultant to British Divers Marine Life Rescue
Lime House, Regency Close, Uckfield, East Sussex TN22 1DS, UK
www.bdmlr.org.uk
International marine animal rescue organisation.

Fran Lockhart
works for the John Muir Trust
Leith Office: 41 Commercial Street, Edinburgh EH6 6JD, Scotland, UK
www.jmt.org
Dedicated to the protection of wild land for nature and people.

Francis Rossi
The legendary rock star
www.statusquo.co.uk

Peter C. H. Pritchard
runs the Chelonian Research Institute,
402 South Central Avenue, Oviedo, FL 32765, USA
Chelonianresearch.wordpress.com
Dedicated to the study and conservation of turtles and tortoises in the
world.

Lawrence Anthony
owns Thula Thula Private Game Reserve & Safari Park
P.O. Box 87, Heatonville, KwaZulu Natal 3881, South Africa
www.thulathula.com
Exclusive private game reserve offering luxury African safari lodge
accommodation in the ancestral land of the Zulu king, Shaka.

Sheri Soltes
is the founder of Texas Hearing & Service Dogs
4803 Rutherglen, Austin, TX 78749, USA
www.servicedogs.org
Training and placing hearing and service dogs.

Colleen O'Brien
works for PETA – people for the ethical treatment of animals
501 Front Street, Norfolk, Virginia 23510, USA
www.peta.org

The largest animal rights organisation in the world, focussing on the areas in which the largest numbers of animals suffer the most intensely for the longest periods of time: factory farms; laboratories; the clothing trade; and the entertainment industry. Also works on other issues, including the cruel killing of beavers, birds and other pests, and the abuse of back yard dogs.

Robin Loder
speaks of Leonardslee
Lower Beeding, Horsham West Sussex RH13 6PP, UK
T: 01403 891 212
www.leonardslee.com
One of England's most spectacular gardens, world famous for its rhododendrons and azaleas.

Mary Harboe
is an author and a presenter on Talk Radio Europe
www.talkradioeurope.com

Peter Knapp
owns Parkside Veterinary Surgery
61 Ruskin Road, Carshalton, Surrey SM5 3DD, UK
www.parksidevet.com – for the practice
www.e-vet.com – for veterinarians, animal health professionals and those interested in animal health and welfare.

Ricky Dietz
works at the Audobon Zoo
6500 Magazine Street, New Orleans, LA 70118
www.auduboninstitute.org/zoo.html
Established in 1914 to maintain and develop Audubon Park, celebrating the wonders of nature.

Paula Fasseas

is the founder of PAWS

Chicago Development Office, 1110 W. 35th Street, Chicago, IL 60609, USA

www.pawschicago.org

The city's largest no-kill humane organisation, offering clinics, education, resources, advocacy programmes and contacts.

Adam M. Roberts

works for Born Free, USA united with API

1122 S Street Sacramento, CA 95811, USA

www.bornfreeusa.org

With a mission to end the suffering of wild animals in captivity, rescue individual animals in need, protect wildlife – including highly endangered species – in their natural habitats, and encourage compassionate conservation globally.

Ray Hale

is the co-founder of the Cambridge Pet Crematorium

A505 Main Road, Thriplow Heath, nr Royston, Hertfordshire SG8 7RR, UK

T: 01763 207700

www.cpccares.com

Established in 1979, CPC is a family-owned business offering a wide range of pet cremation services to bereaved pet owners.

Jo-Ann Dono

works for the Blue Cross

Shilton Road, Burford, Oxon OX18 4PF

www.bluecross.org.uk

One of the UK's oldest animal welfare charities and provides veterinary care for the pets of people who cannot afford the fees of private vets.

Jo-Ann Dono also works for the Society of Companion Animal Studies

www.scas.org.uk

Promoting the study of human-companion animal interactions and raising awareness of the importance of pets in society.

Universities Federation for Animal Welfare (UFAW)
The Old School, Brewhouse Hill, Wheathampstead,
Hertfordshire AL4 8AN, UK
T: 01582 831818
www.ufaw.org.uk
Uses scientific knowledge and established expertise to improve the welfare
of animals as pets, in zoos, laboratories, on farms and in the wild.

Kinky Friedman
More about this versatile singer, writer, politician, animal lover *et al* at
www.kinkyfriedman.com

Jenny Seagrove
This lovely star of stage and screen is most proud of her work for charities
which include The Horse Refuge, Dobell Farm, Moons Green, Wittersham,
Tenterden, Kent TN30 7PR.
www.thehorserefuge.org

Warren Eckstein
More about this celebrated pet expert and humorist at www.thepetshow.com

Sara Rapoport
More about this artist on www.sararapoport.co.uk

Susie Cornfield
More about this writer at www.susiecornfield.com

and not forgetting . . .

Brains the MagnifiCat
who was rescued from the street and brought into the author's life by the
UK's largest feline welfare charity – Cats Protection, National Cat Centre,
Chelwood Gate, Haywards Heath, Sussex RH17 7TT, UK
www.cats.org.uk

Your Special Animal

The following blank pages are here for you to write about your animal, perhaps to include a picture. Feel free to use (or ignore) these ideas which might remind you of special memories:

Animal's name

Breed

Colouring

Physical distinguishing marks

Age

Origin

Habits

Likes

Dislikes

Cause of death/loss

Special memories

Words, songs or music which remind you of your animal